Eggs are Expensive, Sperm is Cheap

50 Politically Incorrect Thoughts for Men

by Greg Krehbiel

Second Edition

http://crowhill-publishing.com

Cover art by stibeliuz on fiverr.com.

Cover design by pro_ebookcovers.
http://fiverr.com/pro_ebookcovers

Copyright 2014, 2019 by Greg Krehbiel, All rights reserved.

ISBN-13: 978-0692312636
ISBN-10: 0692312633

Introduction

It seems obvious to me, and to many others, that our society is very confused when it comes to the relationship between the sexes. People get rich rapping disgusting lyrics about women. Family courts are terribly unfair to men. And somehow, even the quest to get to Mars is "another example of male entitlement." ("The patriarchal race to colonize Mars is just another example of male entitlement," NBC News, Feb. 21, 2018.)

It's beyond crazy.

The point of this little book is to outline a different perspective. I don't know you, or your background, or what you've been exposed to, but I can guess that what I'm going to say isn't what you've been hearing all your life. And let me warn you right now — you won't agree with it all. That's perfectly okay. Six months from now, when I re-read this, I probably won't agree with it all either.

Think of this book as a collection of thoughts to challenge and stretch your mind. I didn't receive them from an angel or translate them from a stone tablet. On the other hand, I was sober the entire time I wrote this, and I've been thinking about these issues for a very long time, so it's probably not all bad. And if you read the reviews, other people like it too.

I want to be straight with you up front. The "politically correct" will hate what I'm saying here. People with modern sensibilities may sneer at these ideas. Oprah would probably abhor every word of it. But that's okay. And the reason it's okay is that it's pretty obvious that we're on the wrong path and need a change. Perhaps some of these thoughts can help you form your own ideas.

There are a few things this book is not, which I'd like to clarify right now.

First, this is not a scholarly work and I'm not trying to prove anything. I don't expect you to be convinced. I don't even expect you to understand. All I hope to do is to plant some seeds in your mind of a different perspective on sex roles.

Second, there are people who, when they have an idea, want to impose it on everybody else through the law. That's not my goal at all. I'm merely trying to get another voice out into the conversation. I don't have the power or the desire to force anybody to adopt any of these ideas.

Third, this book is not meant to be any sort of judgment on you, or your friend, or your crazy ex-lover, or on anybody else. If you live your life a different way, fine. Take the path that makes you happy. I'm not here to lay a guilt trip on you.

My goal is to expose you to another perspective so that it floats around in your brain for a while. I hope that as you observe things in the real world, from time to time this perspective will leap out of your memory and say, "there! See that? Maybe that crazy guy had a point."

Here's the bottom line. I think our society has gone nuts when it comes to sexual morality, and I think a more traditional view would be better for everybody. I think this is incredibly obvious, if you take the time to think about it and observe the world around you, but I also think we're all under a lot of social pressure to suppress those thoughts.

I suspect that you've been conditioned to think of "traditional morality" as constricting, oppressive and no fun. You probably assume that it's only because of religion that people believe in or follow traditional morality. I would like to suggest that traditional morality — in its broad outlines, anyway — is entirely rational, is in tune with who you really are as a human being, and that following it is better for you and for everybody else. And when I say "better," I also mean more fulfilling.

If you live in 21st century America, you've been steeped in a very ideologically-driven approach to the issues I'm going to discuss. You got it from the entire culture — from your friends and your colleagues, TV and movies, books, school, parents and pastors. There's a saying that a fish doesn't know he's wet. It's such an assumed part of his surroundings that he doesn't think about it. In a similar way, we don't stop to think about a lot of the assumptions that we breathe in along with the air. Our environment soaks us in the modern myth about sex and sex roles, and we don't stop to think critically about it.

I'd like to help you get your mind outside of this modern myth, at least for a little while, and think about things from a different perspective. I'm going to offer 50 thoughts (the bold, bulleted points). The purpose is simply to get that alternative viewpoint somewhere in your brain. I'll explain each of the points in a little bit of detail, but I think that as you read through them, you'll start to get the broader picture. And if you're interested in pursuing the topic further, I'll mention some other resources you might consider.

Part 1 — The Theoretical Foundation

• A lot of what you know about men and women is wrong

Well-meaning, friendly, intelligent, loving people have very likely been deceiving you all your life on the subject of male-female relations. They didn't do this out of malice, but because they've been steeped in an ideological agenda that has influenced almost everything and everyone. That ideological agenda has a lot of errors, but as I see it there are three big ones.

1. Men and women are essentially the same.

2. Women have historically been oppressed by the patriarchy and are finally coming into the freedom they deserve.

3. Men and women have equal rights, except when women don't like that.

This agenda has other errors that we'll get into, but those seem like the big three. And by the way, "it seems to me" is exactly how you should read everything in this little book. That's all this is — my opinion, based on my observations. If it helps you to think through these issues, fine. If not, …. Well, after you've thought about it for a while we can sit down and discuss it over a beer.

I'm not a scientist, and I try to avoid the temptation of believing that because I read an article about science, I am therefore "following the science," or that my views are "based on science." That's self-congratulatory nonsense. At best I could say that my views are influenced by somebody who thinks his views are based on science. And even that might be a stretch.

It's important to remember that most of the things you think you know, you only know because someone told you. Maybe it's time for someone to tell you different.

Along those lines, here's a very interesting thread on things that science supposedly shows about sex differences.

https://twitter.com/SteveStuWill/status/1062662607285379072

I am 100% confident that ABC news could find a panel of women's studies professors who would take issue with each of these things, and claim the science is on their side. Whatever. I'm not trying to convince you that the science is on my side. I'm only trying to convince you that there is another side, and it's worth considering.

A wise man once said, "the first to present his case seems just, until another comes along and examines him." That's why a trial has a prosecuting attorney and a defense attorney. You can't expect to know the truth if you only listen to one side of the story. Generally speaking, you've only heard one side about sex. I'm going to try to give you another way of looking at it.

• Eggs are expensive, sperm is cheap

That might strike you as slightly rude, and it might seem like an odd place to start, but that is the fundamental thing you need to know. Almost everything else flows from that fact. It's the rule that governs species that reproduce the way we do, and once you grasp that concept and start to think about its implications, you'll start to understand male and female behavior in a different way. You'll also start to understand why the modern view is inconsistent with human nature.

"Sperm is cheap" because the man makes it all the time, and donating some of it doesn't inconvenience him in the slightest. "Eggs are expensive" because the woman only has a limited number of them, they're only available one at a time (as a general rule), only at certain times of the month, and if one of them is fertilized it uses up an enormous amount of the woman's resources. It also changes her life substantially — for a long time. That is, procreation is a huge investment for her, but a very small investment for him.

From this simple fact alone, it should be clear that men and women have different interests when it comes to sex and mating. It's like a poker game were the ante for men is one leaf, and the ante for women is five ounces of gold. Men and women have very different stakes in the game. And since they have such different stakes, why should we expect them to have the same desires, or to behave in the same way?

The biologists tell us that every creature has an interest in passing on its genes. That's the genius of Richard Dawkins' *The Selfish Gene.* If you look at a creature as if its goal is to pass on its genes, things make a lot more sense.

The anthropomorphism inherent in that mindset is just a useful fiction. Creatures aren't consciously planning to pass on their genes. The idea is that if some species doesn't do a good job of passing on its genes, that species wouldn't survive long. And, contrariwise, it's helpful to look at it from the other direction as well. The creatures that have survived have learned to be effective at passing on their genes.

It isn't a conscious thing. It's not as if a banana wants to make other banana plants. But banana plants that are better suited to making other banana plants are the ones that pass along their genes to the next generation and stick around.

The same is true of humans. If you had a race of humans that didn't want to reproduce, they wouldn't be around for long. Again, to look at it from the other direction, the creatures that are around for a long time are the ones that have optimized their reproductive strategy — at least in comparison to their competition.

Here's the important point. The optimal strategy for a man to pass on his genes will be different than the optimal strategy for a woman. Males want to pass on their genes given the reality that their sperm is cheap. Females want to pass on their genes knowing that their eggs are expensive.

Don't feel as if you need to grasp that completely right now. I'll be coming back to the theme throughout the book, and it should become clearer as we move along.

Also, don't think that men or women sit around pondering the question of how to pass on their genes, or even give the matter much thought at all. The point is not that we think about such things, or are even aware of them. The point is that this underlying reality affects us, often subconsciously. In a sense, we are machines built and designed to do precisely one thing – pass on our genes. And everything else is icing.

We humans have lots of strange desires and instincts and preferences that we aren't aware of, and that we often don't understand. We often don't know why we have them.

For example, men prefer women with long hair, and women (at certain times of the month) prefer men with strong jaws. Men don't think, "Gee, which of those women over there has the best chance of passing along my genes? Oh, I know. It's the ones with long hair!" Rather, the men who have certain preferences (e.g., for women with long hair) have been more successful, so those preferences have survived.

Why? What does long hair have to do with anything?

It doesn't, really. It's a proxy for good health. A man can't see "good health," but he can see long hair, and if a woman with long hair is more likely to be healthy, then preferring women with long hair means he's more likely to mate with healthy women.

Acting out these strange hints about reproductive success is part of the story, but it's not the whole story. It's not as if men and women are independent actors, living out in the world all on their own. Humans live with other humans, and a strategy that might seem successful from the man's point of view isn't going to work if it doesn't also work from the woman's point of view, because it takes two to tango.

Successful human societies have to deal with the realities of male and female biology and create rules to make these two different interests work together for the common good. In order to understand the relationship between the sexes, you need to understand the man's interests, the woman's interests, and the interests of human society in general.

• Females and males are fundamentally different in important ways

Most of us learned in elementary school that lionesses do most of the hunting for the pride. Why do lionesses do that? Is that because of the books their mothers read to them when they were cubs? Or maybe because of the social expectations lion society imposed on them?

Nobody thinks that for a second. We all recognize that female lions are somehow wired to behave differently than male lions. It's their nature.

We're surrounded by examples of sex differences in animals, but we often think the same rules don't apply to humans. Why is that? In a way, the weird modern attitudes towards sex and sex roles is a strange kind of creationism. Animals are one way, but humans are completely different.

A male robin doesn't behave the same as a female robin. That's not because some patriarchy of robins has forced the female robin into a subservient position. It's because the species was more successful when the female robins behaved one way and the male robins behaved another way. It was a matter of maximizing resources ... or, I don't know. Something. I'm no expert on robins, and the mechanics don't matter. What matters is that robins got along better when the males behaved one way and the females behaved another way. And the pope had nothing to do with it.

Somewhere in our recent history, we humans got the strange notion that what's normal and expected in the animal kingdom doesn't apply to us, and that different sex roles among humans were created by evil forces and harshly imposed upon us by ancient manifestations of Jerry Falwell. We're often expected to believe that if it weren't for these evil cultural forces imposing these sexist rules on us, men and women would be the same. They'd play with the same toys in the nursery and they'd seek the same jobs when they're adults.

Why in the world would we think such a thing? Why would we think we're exempt from what we see all over the animal kingdom?

Doesn't it make more sense to think that different gender roles are part of who we are as men and women? We've already seen that men and women have fundamentally different interests in sex because of the relative abundance of sperm and the relative scarcity of eggs. Why would we expect men and women to behave like each other?

Just take a look at what you know and see every day. Men and women are clearly different in many physical ways. On average, men are bigger and stronger than women. Have you ever stopped to wonder why? By the time you finish this book I think you'll have a good guess.

The modern notion is that these things are just funny happenstance, and that men and women are mostly interchangeable mentally and socially, so the same rules and social expectations should apply to both sexes. The modern sexual catechism says we don't want to have a "double standard" about male and female behavior.

As a silly example of this insistence on male-female parity, consider the sense of smell. I've been a home brewer for about 32 years. I've met a lot of home brewers in that time, and as a general rule my experience has been that men like the smell of the malt, the hops, and the whole brewing process, but their wives and girlfriends hate it and want the men to brew outside. That's not universal by any stretch (there are lots of female home brewers), but it seems very common.

A couple times when I have mentioned this observation, people have taken offense at the very idea that men and women would have different preferences about smells. They think I'm some sort of Neanderthal for even suggesting such a thing.

How did we get to such a crazy place? Male dogs behave differently than female dogs. Male frogs behave differently than female frogs. Every bartender knows that men and women have different tastes. Why is it offensive to suggest that men and women might have different reactions to the smells of home brewing? It's not rational, it's just a silly ideological bias.

An article in *National Geographic* recently reported, "Females are better at discriminating among colors, researchers say, while males excel at tracking fast-moving objects and discerning detail from a distance—evolutionary adaptations possibly linked to our hunter-gatherer past."

We've developed this weird ability to realize there are sex differences, and then pretend there are no sex differences. It's a form of cultural madness.

Some studies suggest that males have better spatial and motor abilities, but females have better memory and understand social situations better.

What's fascinating is how easily the results of the studies are tossed aside if they affirm a familiar stereotype. It's as if we start with the assumption that long-held sexual stereotypes are false, then automatically discount any evidence that supports them. Why do we do that?

There is, of course, some legitimate concern that such differences will be used to justify discriminatory behavior. E.g., women in general are this way, therefore this particular woman is this way. Which is, of course, a misuse of statistics. Groups characteristics don't define an individual.

More often than not, however, legitimate research on sex differences is rejected *a priori* as a sin against an ideological agenda.

According to the modern view, if it weren't for the distorting influence of the evil patriarchy, we should expect an equal number of male and female engineers and an equal number of male and female nurses. In the modern view, there's nothing about men that makes them more likely to be engineers and nothing about women that makes them more likely to be nurses. Those kinds of differences are all a result of social pressure – and a lack of funding for progressive policies.

This stuff astonishes me. Where do we get such crazy ideas? The notion that men and women should be equal in all respects is incredibly odd. Yet we've all been pressured into assuming it. We've intentionally blinded ourselves to the possibility of sex differences and different sex roles, and we regard any suggestion of significant differences between the sexes as offensive and prejudicial. To mention the possibility is enough to get you fired from a job. Especially in academia.

Give yourself permission to question the prevailing ideology.

Once you take off the blinders and admit that men and women might be different, the notion that men are women are *not* different strikes you as one of the stupider things you've ever heard, and you wonder how you could have ever believed it.

I should emphasize again, however, that differences in general populations should not be used to discriminate against individuals. Even if it's true (and it is true) that men *as a group* have characteristics that make them more likely to be engineers, and women *as a group* have characteristics that make them more likely to be nurses, that does not mean that a woman can't be a fantastic engineer or a man can't be a fantastic nurse.

• Men have historically sacrificed to protect and defend women

I know that sounds crazy and out of place, but please bear with me. It fits.

You've probably been taught all your life that men have been dragging women around by their hair, beating them with clubs and raping them in caves. Not literally, of course, but that men are like that and would behave that way if they could. As far as a man is concerned (so we're told), a woman is just an object to be used.

When men got their hands on better technology, they kept their wives barefoot and pregnant in the kitchen, or forced them to stay at home and watch soap operas so they wouldn't mess up the old boy network back at the office.

According to the modern mythology, it's only in the last 100 years that we're beginning to recover from the dark ages of patriarchy. Women are finally throwing off the shackles and taking their rightful place in society. They've been oppressed for so long, and light is finally dawning. (Cue "The Age of Aquarius.")

Please take a moment to consider this other possibility.

For most of human history, life has been awful for everybody. Yes, of course it was bad for women. It was also bad for men, who were (just for example) grabbed out of their parents' home and forced to serve as soldiers in the king's army — whether they wanted to or not. Or they were dragged off the dock and forced to serve in the navy, where they lived in horrible conditions, ate horrible food, and were beaten mercilessly for any disobedience.

The thing you have to understand is that there was a kind of dread calculus to the nastiness of life. Remember the fundamental lesson: eggs are expensive and sperm is cheap. A society can afford to lose a lot of its men. It can't afford to lose many of its women or children. Consequently, societies that *sacrifice men to protect women and children* are more likely to survive. That's why men fight the wars and go downstairs in their underpants to check out the weird sound in the basement.

Men (as a group) are physically, mentally and emotionally suited to these tasks because — all together now — sperm is cheap and eggs are expensive. It's better for humanity in general for men to be the cannon fodder, so appropriate mental and physical characteristics were selected for in the male gene pool.

The lionesses may do most of the hunting for the pride, but when it comes to a fight, the lion is the king. He has the size and the talent. And no amount of "you go girl" talk to the lionesses is going to change that.

Sex differences in humans may have a cultural component, and some of them may be entirely cultural. But it's un-scientific (and generally ridiculous) to rule out the possibility that *some* sex differences are biological. We should take it as a given that at least some sex differences in humans are no more a matter of culture than the sex roles of robins or bears or goats are a matter of culture. Our closest cousins in the animal world have sex difference. Why shouldn't we?

What un-natural magic has caused humans to be sexually egalitarian? (Again, often it seems we believe some twisted kind of creationism.)

There are some things about humans that are different, of course. While other creatures do many things, or even most things, by instinct, more of our activity involves conscious intent. I'll discuss this more later, but the instincts that allowed humanity to survive also worked themselves into successful social structures. These structures were created to protect the society, and especially to protect women and children, usually *at the expense of men.*

History is not a story of men oppressing women. Yes, of course, some men oppressed some women. But as a general rule, the man's part has been to sacrifice himself to protect and save women and children.

• Office work is not more fulfilling or meaningful than keeping house and raising a family

If you compare the life of the successful New York City ad exec to the life of a woman caught at home in a loveless marriage, ironing shirts for a man she despises, then yes, I suppose office work might be more meaningful or fulfilling than keeping house and raising kids. That's how the lie that women would be happier if they got jobs outside the home got started. You're supposed to compare the best of office life with the worst of home life.

Before I go on, please pause here for a quick clarification. In no way am I trying to disparage women who choose to work, or choose not to have children. That's not the message at all. People are free to make their own decisions. But while there may have been an assumption in the past that women will stay home and raise kids, now the assumption is the opposite, and there are people in our society who want to disparage women who choose that life. They look down on such people, and belittle their choices.

The people who try to shame women who choose to put kids and family first seem to despise traditional femininity and to only value what men have historically done. It's as if they can only see value in (what was) the man's role.

It was a horrible, stupid, misguided idea.

To try to get some perspective, what if we compare the man who has to work a hard job in the factory all day — or in a coal mine — to the mom who gets to stay home and take care of the kids? I happen to love kids and think they're a joy, and the satisfaction of seeing a little child grow into a responsible and happy adult is a million times better than anything work can offer.

But forget my personal experience. What do people in the real world choose to do when they have a choice? When women actually get to do what they want to do, what do they choose?

You would think – if you came from one side of the ideological divide – that the more egalitarian a society became, and the more people were freed from economic or cultural pressure to conform to stereotypes, the more they would make similar choices. That is, without people telling women to be nurses and men to be engineers, you'd get more female engineers and more male nurses.

The opposite is the case. In the countries that are ranked the highest for eliminating such pressure and allowing people to make the choices they want to make, people make *more traditional choices*, not less, and men and women exhibit more personality differences. (If you don't believe me, search for something like "the gender equality paradox," or "more egalitarian societies women choose more traditional roles.")

Organizations that claim to be acting for women aren't advocating what women actually want. They have things quite backwards, and surveys consistently show this. Most women want to have kids and a family. They're not being forced into that by the evil patriarchy. They feel that way because it's natural for them to feel that way. And most men would love the chance to be able to stay home with their kids more often.

Men aren't the providers because it's such a joy and so empowering to sit at a desk all day. Men act as providers to free up women so they can devote their time to children and family – which is what most women want in life.

If you look at it from a historical perspective, men needed to help women in this way because baby humans are pretty helpless. One odd thing about humans is that we have these very large heads to accommodate our over-sized brains. Our heads are so large that baby humans have to be born before they're fully developed. That is, the size of our heads grew larger and larger, but the escape hatch didn't. I've read this has something to do with the mechanics of walking, but in any event, making a larger birth canal to accommodate these big heads just didn't work, so babies had to be born earlier.

This leaves baby humans pretty helpless and in need of constant care for a long time. The survival of the species requires that women have a safe place to give birth and raise these helpless little tikes. Somebody — not the woman — has to go out into the world and tame the wilderness.

How that came to be called "oppression" is one of the mysteries that sociologists will be studying for centuries.

There has been enormous effort expended over the last few decades to minimize and disrespect the role of house wives and stay-at-home moms and to push women into careers. There's pressure to make women feel guilty if they don't want to be just like men. Despite all this, many women still want to be mothers and many still prefer to spend time at home with the kids. Could it be that patriarchy isn't the right explanation for this? Could it be that women feel the way they do because that's the way they are?

Imagine what the world would be like if the culture actually affirmed family and motherhood?

• Different rules apply to men and women

While listening to CSPAN radio recently I heard Rep. Nancy Pelosi comment on some jerk in the news. Her comment on his behavior was, "This is disrespectful to women."

This is one of the few times I will agree with Nancy Pelosi. The guy's behavior was disrespectful to women. But if you heard the tone of Rep. Pelosi's voice, it was obvious that she expected her statement to end debate right there. If something can be said to be "disrespectful to women" it must be awful, and it must be opposed, right?

Well ... yes, actually. If something is disrespectful to women then it should be opposed. We should respect women, just like we should respect everybody else. But as you'll see, we should especially respect women because .... Quiz time. Why should we especially respect women? You should know by now.

Still, when I heard Rep. Pelosi's comment it made me stop and try to remember the last time I heard someone say "this is disrespectful to men." I have a pretty good memory, and I don't think I have ever heard that phrase.

This is one of the amusing contradictions of the modern view. The modern view says "anything that can be said of men can be said of women and vice versa." You'll notice this assumption creeping up all the time. If you say "women are X," people will immediately say you're sexist because you're implying that something can be said about women that's different from what would be said about men.

Our culture has this crazy idea that anything (other than physical characteristics) that can be said about men can and should be said of women and vice versa. But ... we don't really follow that rule, because we all know that it's nonsense, even when we're not willing to admit it. As an example, nobody says "this is disrespectful to men."

There's a very simple reason why nobody says it. Because nobody would care.

• Successful societies protect women

Why does nobody care if something is disrespectful to men? There's a good and a bad reason.

The good reason is that *we naturally want to protect women* because (you know this) eggs are expensive. Protecting people in general is a good idea, but protecting women is mandatory for the species. It's built into our genes. It's who we are as human beings. It's who we had to be and how we had to learn to behave to survive. If we didn't have an instinct to protect women, we wouldn't have made it. "Women and children first" wasn't because the men wanted to hang around and have another smoke on the sinking ship.

That's why the female perspective matters so much, and *that is a good thing.* The flip side is that for most modern people the male perspective doesn't matter much at all. This is the ugly consequence of the modern agenda, which has been pushing a phony female perspective — generally at the expense of men.

Now, you may be tempted to say, "Well, given what you've been saying all along, isn't it true that the male perspective isn't that important — because sperm is cheap."

Yes and no. It's not quite that simple.

• Successful societies respect men

It's true that men have to be disposable in the service of women and children. While that instinct may develop naturally in some men, the society also has to encourage it. Remember, while robins do things by instinct, we have to think about things. Men have an instinct to protect women, but they also have to be socialized and convinced into it, and part of that socialization is to respect men who take up that role of protecting women. Men have to be given some reason to take on the yoke society needs them to take, otherwise they'll just say never mind and stay home and play X-box all day.

At this point you might be thinking, "you keep talking about this instinct stuff like everybody has the same instincts. Some boys are timid and they grow up into timid men. They would sooner run and hide than stand up for anybody."

Of course, but let's review some basic rules here. There is a difference between generalities and specifics. "Men are stronger than women" is true, even though Suzy is stronger than Sam, because the average man is stronger than the average woman.

We all know that, when we stop to think logically, but we tend to put it aside and pretend it's not true when we hear something that bothers us.

For example, if you're one of those people who believes more women should be in STEM, and you hear somebody say "when given the choice, few women actually choose to be in STEM," you might think, "but I know lots of women who studied STEM."

That may be true, but it's irrelevant. Anecdotes and specific exceptions don't change a general rule.

Back to instincts. I'm certainly not claiming that all men or all women have the same instincts, or that there are instincts that men have that no woman has, or vice versa. That would be dumb.

Think of dogs for a moment. If you go to your favorite search engine and type "dogs that like to swim," the results aren't going to be specific dogs — Rover and Daisy and Molly and Butch. The results are going to be breeds of dogs. English Setter, Chesapeake Retriever, etc.

Does that mean that every single Chesapeake Retriever in the world likes to swim? I'm not a dog expert, but I don't think so. It means that, as a group, that's what they're like. If your Chesapeake Retriever doesn't like to swim, that doesn't change the general statement about the breed.

In the same way, some things can be generally true about men that aren't true of every specific man, and we need to keep that in mind when we're thinking of boys and their instincts.

I'm sure you've seen articles lamenting the fact that men aren't growing up. They're more interested in video games and porn. There are reasons for that, and they're fairly simple. One reason is that sex (real or virtual) is cheap and easily available today, even to losers. But another reason is that men aren't respected in male roles, so why should they bother to become a man?

Let's think back to Rep. Pelosi's remarks. Just for fun, go to your favorite search engine and look for "disrespectful to women" (with the quotes) and look at the number of hits, then search "disrespectful to men" (with the quotes) and compare. The difference is pretty interesting.

It's important to note that there's a difference between "men are disposable" and "the male perspective doesn't matter." Our culture has pushed a distorted, twisted perspective on women's rights. It starts with the wrong-headed assumption that women have been oppressed, that men are the oppressors, and that traditional male virtues are bad things. It continues by encouraging women to take on men's roles, and encouraging men to shut up — or, rather, to sit back and celebrate "women's successes." Women are victims, you see, and men should feel guilty about the past and happy about all the great strides women are finally making.

The way we got to this seems very predictable. We protect and care for women and how they feel, but we really don't care all that much how men feel. Men aren't supposed to get upset at hardships and disappointments. To the contrary, we train them not to. *As we should.*

In that kind of setting, here's what happens. If women complain about how they're treated and how they feel, everybody's concerned because we have an instinct to protect them. *As we should.* If men complain about how they're treated and how they feel we tell them to grow a pair and quit complaining. *As we should.*

You can see the rhetorical imbalance. If there's nothing to counteract that, it's not sustainable. We'd barrel down a path that promotes women's interests and demonizes men, or at least ignores their interests, until the culture collapses around us.

The "protect women" ethic is entirely correct, but it's only sustainable in a society where people accept that men and women are different and have different roles, and that both men and women are *respected in those roles.* Once that no longer applies, there will inevitably be a tendency to interpret everything in light of the woman's perspective.

• The men's rights movement is a mix of good and bad

There's been a reaction to all this foolishness and imbalance in our society, and it generally falls under the category of the "men's rights" movement. Some of it seeks to fix the problems we've created by promoting the myth of equality. Some men's rights activists (MRAs) buy into the essential stupidity of equalitarianism and simply want us to be consistent about it. If the female perspective matters, the male perspective should matter just as much. If women can complain about how they're treated, so can men.

I think that is a misguided approach. The solution is not to try to make equalitarianism work, but to expose it as a lie.

Men and women *should* be treated differently because they are different, and any attempt to change that is an attempt to argue and fight against reality. Reality tends to be a pretty durable thing and usually has the last laugh.

Having said that, MRAs do make some important points. The modern view, which is supposedly based on fairness and treating people the same, isn't actually fair at all. It hides behind a cloak of "equality" when it's convenient, but then takes advantage of our natural desire to protect women when that's more convenient.

The result is that the woman's perspective has been exaggerated way out of proportion and the man's perspective has been ignored. Worse than that, men are regularly portrayed as oafs and morons when they're not being portrayed as rapists, criminals and abusers. And it's very clear why. If women are consistently portrayed as idiots on car commercials, women's groups will complain and it will be on the evening news. If men are consistently portrayed as idiots on car commercials, nothing happens.

This is creating a very dangerous cultural problem. A healthy society recognizes male and female differences and encourages men and women in those roles. The result of the modern silliness is that we don't even believe in sex roles anymore, so very few people are willing to tell men how to be men and women how to be women. Because that's sexist.

Let me be quite clear about this. *It is sexist, and that's a very good thing,* because it's sexist in the right way — that is, it recognizes the differences between the sexes.

Sexism is not a problem. Sexism is a virtue.

• In the modern view, women have rights while men have responsibilities

One perverted result of the modern view of things is that women have more and more rights, but men keep their responsibilities. In some ways this is natural and expected. Society needs to use men to protect women, which is right and proper. But modern folk need to decide which way it's going to be. If we follow the equalitarian idea, then men and women should have the same sorts of rights and responsibilities. If we're not going to follow the equalitarian nonsense, then we have to decide what's appropriate for men and what's appropriate for women.

We're not doing either of those things, so we have a confused mess.

As an illustration of women's rights and men's responsibilities, consider that most fundamental aspect of male-female interaction — making a baby.

Let's assume a healthy couple has consensual sex. If the woman gets pregnant, she has the right to have an abortion, to keep the baby, or to give the baby up for adoption. The man has the responsibility to be ruled by the woman's decision. No one can force a woman to become a mother, but the woman can force the man to become a father.

You may be thinking. "She's not forcing him to become a father. If he didn't want to become a father, he should have kept his zipper closed." I happen to agree with that sentiment, and that would be the right answer in the context of a traditional view of sex and sex roles. But we don't live in that world.

Isn't it strange that it's okay to say "if you didn't want a kid you should have kept your zipper closed" to the man, but no one would dare say the same thing to the woman? Women's rights advocates would scream bloody murder. According to the modern dogma, the woman has every right to have sex whenever she wants, and she has every right to decide – anywhere along the way – to change her mind about having a baby. The man's rights end at the choice to have sex.

Even though the man doesn't have as many rights, he does retain the *obligation* to provide child support – if the woman chooses to keep the child. This is a leftover from the traditional concept of the man being responsible for his family.

Women's rights vs. men's responsibilities is a common result of a lot of the crazy things we do these days, and as you tune your ear to it, you'll hear it again and again. It shows up in many places.

As another example, women now have the right to join the armed forces, but men have the responsibility to register for the draft.

In a different context – not as a legal matter, but as a societal expectation – wives have the right to work, or to stay at home, or to come up with their own combination of the two. Men have the responsibility to work to support the family.

The story is often the same. We're very worried about women's rights, and if that imposes some responsibility on men – well, that's what men are there for.

• Male obligations have been re-branded as "privileges"

Over the last hundred years or so, all the male obligations and burdens that were imposed because of the fundamental rule (sperm is cheap) have been very cleverly spun to sound like a male privilege and a sign of the oppression of women.

The male obligation to go out into the world and earn a living — usually away from his wife and children — was cast as some sort of male privilege. Nobody thought to ask men whether they would rather be spending time with the family, because the male perspective doesn't matter. Men are the providers, so suck it up and go dig some coal.

A recent article in Quillette by Jerry Barnett illustrates this phenomenon.

> Working as a photographer for a charity a few years back, I was travelling through Malawi and stopped overnight in a mining town. It was a Wednesday, and I headed out to a bar. Other than a woman serving, everyone else there was male. Some were playing pool. Some were drinking, but

> most were doing neither. I asked the bargirl why there were no women in the place. With a look that suggested I was being dim, she explained: "The men get paid on Friday."
>
> On the surface, in a mining town, the gender pay gap is huge, with the vast majority of money officially going to men. And yet, by Saturday morning, much of the cash has been transferred to bar owners, prostitutes, girlfriends, and wives. A privileged observer might suggest that women in such a town ought to be liberated to earn their own money. But the point is that they already are. While most fair-minded people would no doubt agree that women should be free to take mining jobs if they choose, it's unlikely that many women want such gruelling, dangerous, and unhealthy work when being a bar prostitute, a girlfriend, or a wife to a miner is available as an alternative.

(From "The Price of Sex," November 14, 2019.)

The men have the "privilege" of working in the mine. Lovely.

That does not mean the women have it easy, or that this is a situation to be emulated. I, for one, don't want women to have to earn their living on their back. But the men and the women are making their own choices here, and it's ridiculous to call one choice "privilege."

In the modern, western world, we've done something similar. If a woman thinks she would be more fulfilled by being out in the working world, she should be able to do that. Or stay at home. Or whatever. And somehow the man is the privileged one.

Another example is warfare. If you understand the fundamental math (eggs are expensive and sperm is cheap) you understand why it makes perfect sense to have men fight the wars. Nature seems to understand that because it made the men physically equipped for the task. But somebody who is an absolute genius at spin has convinced us all that this very fact — that it's the men who have to fight and die in war — is now seen as *oppression of women*. It's an unbelievably stupid concept, but we're so immersed in nonsense that it seems to make some kind of sense to modern ears.

You may have been tempted to think that way yourself, and you saw the exclusion of women from various roles in the military as a left-over of pro-male prejudice. You may have thought, "Why can't a woman go fight if she wants to?"

And there you have the female imperative. "If she wants to." The man might be drafted against his will and sent off to fight and die in a war a thousand miles away from everyone he loves for a cause he doesn't believe in. But the woman gets to choose if she wants to fight, and the entire military structure has to be retooled and reorganized to accommodate her preference.

I'm only barely scratching the surface on these issues to give you a sense of how crazy things are. If these thoughts sink in at all, you'll start to see more examples yourself as you read the news and observe the world around you. Other people have elaborated on them in more detail, and I will mention some other resources to consider at the end of this book. For now, I just want to mention these things to start to bend your brain in a different direction.

• "Women were historically oppressed" is an exaggeration

In the modern world, it's hard not to assume the feminist interpretation of most stories. So, for example, if someone were to tell you that China's one-child policy has resulted in a preference for little boys (little girls are often killed or abandoned), you probably assume that's because boys are preferred and valued while girls are not.

"See, patriarchy!" And that probably plays a role.

But there's a factor you may not have considered. Boys in China are expected to provide for their parents in their old age. Girls are not. So, this "male privilege" is also a male obligation.

Please don't get me wrong. The murder of these little girls is a crime that should be stopped. My point here is simply to mention that the motivation behind this outrage might not be what you thought it was. Yes, boys are "privileged." They are privileged with the obligation to care for their parents, so parents have an incentive to want a boy child. To make it even worse, the parents are obligated to care for a girl if she can't (or decides not) to get married. So, if you're only going to have one child, you really want it to be a boy.

Some people want you to believe that everything comes down to "boys are privileged because of patriarchy." Well, if by "patriarchy" you mean an obligation to protect and provide, then yes. Boys are "privileged" precisely because they have the corresponding *obligations*.

Would it all the better if these obligations were shared equally, *i.e.,* if parents had to provide for male and female children when they're grown, and if male and female children both had to provide for elderly parents?

Perhaps that would be better, if we lived in some fantasy world where boys and girls are interchangeable and it's just a matter of assigning the right roles to make everything work out correctly. But that's a delusion. Boys and girls are not interchangeable. Boys and girls are different in important ways. Boys naturally have impulses that girls do not, and vice versa, and the idea that we can change that with different rules or different social norms is, quite simply, nuts.

Some people want a society based on the interchangeability of the sexes. Whatever applies to men applies to women and vice versa. But is the idea even plausible? Is it reasonable to believe that male homo sapiens and female homo sapiens can just be swapped out and moved around and shuffled into the same roles — with no bad consequences? You can't do that with most other animals. Why should we believe that we can do it with humans?

This modern myth that men and women are interchangeable can't be enforced consistently because it runs into this difficult thing called reality. The species didn't develop under the microscope of a feminist legal system, but under the harsh rule of nature, red in tooth and claw. To deal with the difficult realities of life, men had to behave one way and women another. It's part of who we are, and it's not going to change suddenly because somebody thinks that would be more fair.

As another example of rights and obligations, the assumption used to be that men were financially, legally and morally responsible for their children. That meant the men used to get custody of children in a divorce. Note the logic – if you're responsible to care for the child, you get custody of the child. But when that *obligation* was cleverly spun into a privilege, it was called "patriarchy," and we accepted the primacy of the woman's perspective and switched things around. Now women usually get custody of children in a divorce, but men retain the obligation to support them.

How is that fair?

Just for fun, let's pretend we actually are interested in fairness and let's imagine how that might work.

Today, if a woman gets pregnant, she can decide to abort the child, keep it and raise it on her own, or give it up for adoption. She can also choose whether she wants to force the man to pay child support. He has no say in any of her choices, although of course he can contest child support in court. And probably lose.

Let's switch things around and make the child the legal responsibility of the man and see how that might play out.

The woman would still have the right to an abortion, to give the child up for adoption or to keep it and raise it herself. All she has to do is make no claim about who the father is, and that would be that. The child is hers.

However, if she wanted to get child support, she would have to identify the father, and then he would have legal custody of the child. He could choose to take the child into his home. He could choose to pay the woman to raise the child (i.e., child support). Or he could offer to marry the woman.

Just in terms of simple fairness, doesn't that make more sense?

(As an aside, I'm not making a statement about whether abortion is good or bad. I'm simply recognizing it as a reality of modern life.)

• The modern lie, which was supposed to help women, has actually hurt them

The modern confusion often disguises itself as a voice for women, but surveys show that women are actually *less happy* today than they were before all these "voices for women" started changing the rules.

My internal cynic says this makes perfect sense. If you're in the business of trying to make women happier, you really don't want them to be happy — then you lose your market. What you want to do is design a scheme that *seems* to make them happy, and sounds like it will make them happy, but actually makes them miserable. Demand for your product will only increase.

No, I don't believe women's advocates are actually that monstrous. I'm sure they think they're acting in women's best interests. They're just wrong.

Our society has a tendency to start with an assumption ("convincing women to be more like men will make them happier"), then trying it ("focus on your career and don't depend on a man"), and then when it has the *exact opposite effect* of what was expected, we don't dare to wonder if our assumption might have been wrong – because that would be heresy. Rather, we figure we're not trying hard enough and need to double down on our efforts to implement the new reality.

There are lots of ways that women have been misled. They've been told that they have been oppressed, that they are victims, that they would be happier if they acted like men, that motherhood is not fulfilling, and that they are entitled. But there's another one I want to call attention to, and that's the idea that young women should focus on their career and delay marriage.

The truth nobody wants to face is that women are at the top of their game when they're in their 20s. At that point they are the rock stars of the sexual marketplace and they have their best chance of finding a mate. They are also more fertile and more likely to bear healthy children.

After age 30, their market value starts to decline and their chances of attracting a decent man decrease. If they're divorced, the odds get even worse. And if you add kids to the equation, the odds get really bad.

This is harsh language, and I certainly don't mean to insult or discourage anyone who is in that situation. That isn't the point. I wish everybody the best life they can possibly live, and just because things might work out a certain way on average doesn't mean it will work out that way for you.

The problem is that women are being fed a diet of Eat, Pray, Love, and they have this romantic notion that very improbable things are "just going to work out." It's like not saving for retirement and then hoping something magic will come along and save you in the end.

Here's the reality. Women who focus on their careers miss their best chance to get their best possible mate, and they miss their best chance to start a family. I'm not saying women can't choose a career or that they have to start a family. They can do whatever they like. But they have to realize there are trade-offs, and they have to be realistic about them. Nobody can have everything, and efforts to convince women to have a career and then a family are probably not helping anybody.

There's an old saying that women are the gatekeepers of sex while men are the gatekeepers of commitment. To put that another way, women trade sex to get love while men trade love to get sex. While there's some truth to both of those statements, the mixed up modern world has messed with the math.

If you want to do a trade, you want to make the deal while your commodity has some value. Excuse me for this crude analogy, but you get the best money for your horse when it's still young and strong. In the same way, if a man is interested in a woman with whom he can have a family, the woman's value is sky high when she's 23, but by the time she's 33 it's a tougher sale.

Modern people get confused about this, since an older woman is superior in many ways, and many women continue to be quite attractive well past 33.

Which is to miss the point entirely. Men's sexual instincts weren't invented by *Cosmopolitan* magazine in 2019. They developed over millennia, in far different circumstances, and the operating rule was to make babies. From that point of view, a wealthy, wise, interesting and very sexy 50 year old is not nearly as valuable as a 23 year old. Whether we like it or not, a younger woman is a better choice for raising a family.

Modern women have been taught that they can't and shouldn't rely on men. They have to focus on their career and be independent. That means they have to eschew long-term relationships during their peak years, in college and in their 20s, and then maybe think about marriage in their 30s, or even later. What they're not told is that by the time they're done playing career — and probably sleeping around — their market value has plummeted. It will be harder to find the man they want. It will be harder to get pregnant, and they will be less likely to have healthy children.

I know this sounds harsh. I didn't create this situation, I'm just commenting on it.

Women who want a family would be best served by selling when the market is high — that is, to get married early, while they're still young and attractive and have the ability to raise healthy kids.

I know how this sounds. I know some people will be offended. I'm sorry about that. But I didn't write the biological clock, and even if advances in medical technology allow women to have children into their 50s, our basic prejudices and instincts might not change to accommodate that new situation. Men are probably still going to be more attracted to younger women.

Men and women have both been sold a rotten bill of goods in the modern world, and we all need to take a breather and re-evaluate our assumptions. The most important thing is not to fall into the ugly extremes – the man-hating woman or the woman-hating man. Men are not the bad guys. Women are not the bad guys. We're all just trying to adjust to a new world, and so far we're not doing a terribly good job.

This book is mostly written for men, so here's an important takeaway for my male readers. First, don't fall into the trap of blaming women for the world's craziness. There's a lot of that in the so-called "men's rights" movement. It's ugly, it's wrong, and it won't do you any good. Second, if you want to have a family, you need to find a wife who is insulated against a lot of the modern craziness. Good luck finding her. You might have to travel.

• Marriage law was created to protect women

Any successful human society has to address the fundamental math that's been discussed above, namely, that women are essential and men are disposable. The modern confusion has completely ignored that fact and fed us with a storyline about the past that says men were the oppressors and women were oppressed.

That's their spin. This is mine.

Not only does a successful society have to deal with the disposability of the man, it has to address the behavioral side of the problem — that is, how do you convince men to embrace that role?

Above there is a short discussion about instincts, and how men (in general) have an instinct to protect women and children. We all know that's not universal. Some men are selfish cowards. How does society deal with this?

Since sperm is cheap, and since men aren't as naturally invested in children, a successful society tries to create rules that harness the male sex drive and use it to build a culture that protects women and children. One way to do that is to push men towards marriage.

How do you do that? One very effective way is to enforce a rule that the only legitimate way to get sex is within marriage. That does an amazing job of motivating men to do what they have to do to be "marriage material."

Traditional marriage law makes the man responsible for the protection and provision of his wife and kids, which is a benefit to the women and children so long as the guy fulfills his end of the bargain.

If you think about it, the whole thing is a pretty scary proposition — which is why the traditional marriage ceremony says "marriage is not to be entered into unadvisedly or lightly."

The married man doesn't only have to go out and provide for himself — he has to provide for this little society he's creating. And asking a woman to be dependent on a man is a scary thing for her, too. What if he turns out to be a bum? What if he's abusive, or a drunk, or can't hold a job? Those are (unfortunately) realistic fears, and laws and customs were designed to address them.

The dowry is an interesting example of this.

You may have heard that the dowry is a horrible, patriarchal thing, where parents pay some guy to take their daughter off their hand. There may have been some of that, but the real the purpose of the dowry is to provide a fund that a woman can fall back on in if her husband dies, or if things go south in the marriage. That's not always the way it's been practiced, but that's the basic idea behind the concept. It was yet another way that society sought to protect women at the expense of men.

• Monogamy and permanent marriage protects the also-rans

In the state of nature, the alpha males would get most of the women, and the beta males would be scheming for the scraps that fall from the table. That's about how things play out in bars. Or so I'm told.

Socially and legally enforced permanent marriage provides a safe environment for a man and a woman to make a meaningful commitment. A man would be an idiot to invest much of his time or treasure in a marriage if the alpha male one block over can just come and take his wife from him. Or again, from the wife's perspective, she doesn't want to be in a marriage where the husband can easily dump her for a younger model when she's past her prime.

Marriage law was designed to create a stable society, founded on stable families. It protected both men and women from outside threats — the alpha male, the lothario, the seductress — and from the inner threat — from spouses who want to "trade up."

When the man decides to marry, he's making a trade. He exchanges his desire for variety to get stability. The woman is also making a trade. She's relying on a single man, and forsakes her desire to look for somebody better. (As an aside, it's interesting to note that this idea of women dumping the guy and trading up has become a theme in a few TV commercials recently.) The stable relationship created by a traditional family also protects children, and it protects inheritance. All these things keep the wheels on the societal bus because they take the raw material of nature and push it into a relationship that benefits the culture as a whole.

"Traditional morality" is not based exclusively on biology, and it's not based exclusively on some pie in the sky ideal. It evolved over time as the best method to force biological reality into a workable, stable relationship. (But we're so smart we can jettison that and make up our own, better rules, right?)

The protective nature of traditional morality is particularly important for women, because they are pretty vulnerable when they're pregnant or caring for young children. That's not as true in 21st century America as it is in poorer countries, or at earlier times in our history, but you have to remember that our species didn't evolve in the 21st century west. Human nature was crafted well before you could run down to the convenience store to buy baby formula and Pampers, and social and ethical norms – including our moral instincts – developed in that context, not in the modern world.

Looking at in over the long haul of human history, pregnant women needed a lot of help and protection, not just for themselves, but for their young. This was pretty important in our collective past, when both famines and raiding parties were common problems.

Under a traditional marriage, the man trades his earnings for regular access to sex, for the status of being a father and head of the household, and for the chance to have children. He becomes legally, morally and economically responsible for his family, and he has to be willing to lay down his life to protect them.

This bargain creates the engine of a prosperous society, which is families. Families maximize the productive capacity of citizens and create a safe place for the care, socialization and feeding of the next generation. Modern societies are suffering the bad effects of having more and more children who are not raised in stable families. Such children are far more likely to be criminals, or simply not productive.

Marriage provided a way for the average (or below average) guy to get and keep a woman, because the law protected his rights. The law also protected the average (or below average) woman, and her children.

• Men are like dandelions, women are like elephants

Each new generation depends on the success of the members of the previous generation at mating and passing along their genes. That means that each generation is the product of whichever members of the previous generation were better at procreation. So, for example, the plant that is really good at getting its seeds into fertile soil will make more plants of the same kind. Plants whose seeds don't sprout will die off.

How does this apply to men and women?

Imagine two islands. One island is populated by men who like women, and women who like men. The other island is populated by men who prefer video games, and women who would rather read a romance novel than deal with some real fellow. On which island will the humans pass along their genes more effectively?

Of course it's a little more complicated than that. When it comes to this question of passing on genes, men and women have entirely different interests. To illustrate this, think of the generational strategies of the dandelion and the elephant.

The dandelion wants to scatter its seed as far and wide as it can, but it can't do a thing to help those seeds grow. Those little plants in the neighbor's yard are on their own.

The elephant only has one offspring at a time, so it has to invest lots of time and energy to make sure the calf survives.

The male human has the opportunity to adopt a dandelion strategy and spread his seed as far and as wide as he possibly can. He also has the opportunity to act like an elephant, investing time and attention in making sure the child survives to adulthood.

The female human doesn't have any way to pursue the dandelion strategy. As a general rule she can't have more than a few children in her life, so her reproductive strategy has to focus on having a few high-quality offspring that she helps to grow to maturity.

While the man could conceivably have thousands of children (and some men have), the woman will only have a few, or maybe several, and each of them are very costly to her. Having a child is a much bigger investment for the woman than it is for the man, so she has to be more selective. The man doesn't need to be selective because he can rely on the law of averages. If he gets enough seed out there, some of it will sprout.

The woman wants her child to be strong and healthy, so she wants the genes of a strong and healthy male. She is also going to need help nurturing and protecting the child, because she can't do that on her own, and the world is a dangerous place.

Ideally, she would find a strong and healthy man who is also a good protector and provider, but those two needs don't have to point to the same man. She could, for example, mate with the strong and healthy football player but get domestic help from the friendly nerd who knows how to change diapers.

It's all much more complicated than that in real life, but those basic principles set the stage for understanding some of the reasons for sex differences.

For most of human history, men and women have lived in small communities, and they got a lot of support from their little clan, which was mostly made up of their relatives. The people in that little tribe of our ancestors — wandering around on the savannah — didn't only protect or feed their own children, they protected and fed everybody in their little group, because that was good for the clan.

Notice that the clan introduces a third interest in the mating equation, which I will discuss in more detail in the next bullet point.

The man's interest was to spread his seed around as much as possible, but it was also in his interest to make sure at least some of his seed takes root and grows. This doesn't mean that a man consciously wants these things any more than a dandelion wants its seeds to grow. It just means that the man's instincts will push him in that direction.

The woman needs three things: the genes of a healthy man, the protection of a strong man (or men, or a village), and help with care and nurturing. Again, this doesn't mean she's consciously aware of these desires, but her instincts will be pushing her in that direction.

The next question is what the clan wants out of this.

• There's a calculus to traditional marriage

You might think that since the man wants to spread his seed far and wide, it's easy for the woman to find a mate. All she has to do is be available and the guys will come running. But that would be a huge mistake on her part. It's easy for her to attract a man for a night, but if he's the wrong kind of guy, she ends up pregnant and the guy is gone.

Having a child is a big investment for a woman. She needs to play her cards right to get the things she needs — strong genes, protection and help with nurturing and caring for her children. A woman who is simply available has a very good chance of getting pregnant, but not such a good chance that her child will survive, so her genetic line will end right there.

Consequently, the woman wants to attract high-value men with the traits she needs. She does her best to attract, but she also puts up barriers so she can select which men she's interested in.

Clueless men find this confusing, e.g., "If you didn't want men looking at you, or coming on to you, then why did you dress like that?" The obvious answer is that the woman "dressed like that" to attract high-value men. She doesn't want the attention of other, low-value men.

She's not interested in attracting everybody indiscriminately, but it's hard to wear lipstick that only the high-value men can see.

This theory would predict that the natural state of men is to try to get as much sex as they can with as many women as they can — but especially with young, fertile women — and the natural state of women is to be picky about the men they choose. Men will compete to be acceptable to the high-value women, and they will usually compete on matters of material success or physical prowess.

Now let's consider the interests of the clan. If you were trying to design a stable culture with creatures that behave the way I've outlined, how would you do it?

The very last thing you would do is allow the men to get sex on the cheap. One thing that drives men to pursue material success and physical prowess is their desire for access to high-value women. If they can get it some other way, they don't have to worry about being strong or wealthy or intelligent.

That's part of what's wrong with men today. Sex (either real or virtual) is readily available, so ... why do all the work? Why not just stay home and play video games? Why try so hard to make lots of money to impress the high-value women when the college girls are giving it away for a song, and the internet is giving it away for free?

If you want the men in your society to be anything more than lazy bums, you need a system where sex is rare, and where women are choosy about the right things. If the society needs warriors, you want the women to prefer warriors. If society needs industrialists and people who create wealth, you want the women to prefer men who can buy them diamonds and vacations on the Riviera.

An interesting illustration of this phenomenon was the changed attitude the women in New York had towards firefighters and policemen after 9-11.

In any event, the interest of the clan is to use the men's desire for sex to push them towards behavior that is beneficial to society.

Or, in other words, the clan's interest is to say, "not so fast, cowboy. First you have to learn to be a productive member of society."

This is not a great deal for the men. What they want is to get lots of sex on the cheap and then go home to play Nintendo without having to worry about all that hard work and the drama of a "relationship."

This sounds like heresy to modern ears, but traditional sexual morality doesn't only oppress women. It oppresses men as well. It's designed to motivate men to jump through the right hoops before they can have sex, and to limit themselves to one woman.

Under a traditional regime, before he could get a woman into bed the man had to dress nicely to please the woman and her parents. He had to buy flowers. He had to take her to dinner (at his expense). He had to function as her unpaid bodyguard. He had to stop hanging out with his guy friends quite so often (for which he received a lot of abuse) and he had to dote on the woman — because *that's the entrance fee.* There's no guarantee it will work. The man does all this in the hope that he might get the girl.

But think about what society gets out of this! Proper young men who know how to behave, and who are invested in a family.

To seal the deal this poor guy has to agree to be faithful to the girl forever, to support, protect and defend her and any children she has. Then he has to take the higher-paying job he hates so he can be "a good provider" and win the admiration of his wife, of his and her family, and of society.

In the traditional world (think of the days of Sherlock Holmes if that helps) the man's life and ambitions are ordered towards securing this coveted position of husband and father, and society trained men for the necessary mental disciplines, attitudes and sacrifices. (Women were also socialized into their marriage roles, of course.)

To support this whole social model, men were taught that their personal desires are subservient to something that's more important — the family and the nation. They were taught to put the interests of women and children first; even above their own lives. That may mean giving up a seat on a life boat, or charging into gunfire with a bayonet, or it may mean taking a dangerous job to be able to put food on the table and coal in the fireplace. In any event, it meant that his interests came last. There was no way he was going to laze around in his sweats, watch porn and play video games.

The law supported this whole arrangement by drafting only men into the armed forces, by expecting men to take the hard and dangerous jobs, by criminalizing pornography, fornication, prostitution and adultery, and by limiting divorce to very difficult cases.

Society imposed a pretty heavy yoke on the men, and most of it was to secure the safety and security of women and children.

If the man was a laborer, then he was the beast of burden for his family. If he held a professional job, he was his family's "success object," or wage slave. The man took on this yoke for (1) access to sex, (2) the chance of raising a family, (3) the status of being a responsible husband and father, and (4) because it was the morally right thing to do.

In this same context, a social benefit of marriage is that it forces people to get over themselves and think about others. Life is no longer about your own petty wants and needs. For both the husband and the wife, marriage is a kind of schooling in sacrifice and charity.

A lot more could be said about the scope and assumptions of traditional marriage, but that's a general outline, and I think it shows pretty clearly why marriage is on the rocks these days. Each of the four motivating factors I mentioned above are largely irrelevant in modern society.

When you consider marriage from this perspective, do you think it's reasonable to say that men were "privileged"? We're constantly told that all these ancient laws were designed for men's benefit. It seems to me that has it backwards. The rules were designed to restrain men — to break them, tame them and train them — to bend their desires to the service of women and children, and thereby to the culture.

If men had designed the rules they would have come up with something where they got easy access to sex without any strenuous effort. The modern, libertine world is far more of a man's creation than the traditional world was.

The customs and expectations of traditional morality weren't designed to meet men's needs. They were designed to create a stable society *on the backs of men* — where the male sex drive was channeled and directed towards something that benefited the whole culture. The rules maximized the contribution of every man (not just the alpha males), and created stable families.

• Part of our downfall was getting all dogmatic about individual rights

That was a hard section there. If you need to go get a glass of water or something, I'll understand. I'll try to change the pace a little.

I trust you have a basic understanding of how the U.S. government works. For example, you know that every state gets two senators, despite its size.

The state of Rhode Island is about 4,000 square kilometers. Brewster County in Texas is far larger — about 16,000 square kilometers. Brewster County is more than twice the size of Delaware.

Should Brewster County get two senators? As a matter of fairness, why should little Rhode Island get two senators when this great big county in Texas doesn't? Why are we discriminating against those counties?

We're not discriminating *against* those counties, of course. We're discriminating *in favor of* the states.

You could only say that we're being unfair to those large Texas counties if you look at the question in a certain way — that is, if you think that representation in the Senate should be decided by size. (We could do a similar exercise with population, of course, or wealth, or any number of factors.)

The purpose of the Senate is not to represent land mass or population. The Senate is supposed to *represent the states*, which are independent, sovereign entities. Rhode Island is just as much of a state as Texas.

This may seem like a strange background for what I'm about to say, but I'm going to ask you to stretch your brain a bit and think hard on this one. While keeping in mind what I just said about states and representation, can you guess any reason (other than the evil patriarchy) why women didn't get to vote in times past?

Just as with the issue of state representation – with Brewster County vs. Rhode Island – it comes down to the purpose of the representation. The Senate represents the states, despite the fact that they differ in size and population. What does a "voter" represent?

If you're going to design a republic you need to ask a few questions, such as (1) what are the social units and power structures in society?, and (2) how will they be represented in the government? The United *States* obviously has states. It also has congressional districts. We know what they represent. But then we have "voters." What do the voters represent?

The modern answer is fairly obvious. Voters represent individuals. But that wasn't always the only, or the obvious answer. Some people thought that only landowners should vote, because they had more of a stake in the government. Some people today think that illegal aliens should be able to vote. Others think that people on welfare should not be able to vote. A minority view is that you should only be able to vote if you served in some way.

I'm not advocating any particular position, I'm just pointing out that "all individuals get to vote" is not obvious.

Your ideas about voting come down to who you want to be making decisions about the way the country is governed. Every individual? Every productive member? Every law-abiding member?

Just as the Senate represents states, it's easy to imagine situations where voters might represent another key part of society. That could be "landowners," or "workers," or ... "families." Some people say that the family is the basic unit of society.

How might that change your expectation of who can vote? If, for example, the voter represents "families," you might expect that the father (as the head of the family) would vote most of the time, but maybe widows would also vote. There are examples of exactly that in early American history, which should make you think twice about believing that reserving the vote to men was simply based on anti-woman sentiment.

Please don't get me wrong. I'm not arguing against women's suffrage. Nor am I trying to put a happy face on any prejudice that women have been subjected to in the past. What I'm suggesting is that the story you've likely heard all your life — that women weren't allowed to vote because of the evil patriarchy and male privilege — might not be the whole story, and that the fight to allow women to vote was not as simple as you may think.

In the past, all property in a marriage legally belonged to the husband. From a modern point of view, this is automatically interpreted as a statement of what a woman couldn't do — as in "a woman couldn't own property or sign legal documents." Yes, but what is conveniently left out is the other side of the equation. It was also an obligation placed on men. The man was legally responsible for everything the family did — sometimes to the point where men owed the taxes on the wife's income. And if the wife got into debt, that was the man's problem. (There are stories of women intentionally getting into debt to get rid of their husbands via debtor's prison.)

At the time the suffragettes were trying to get the vote for women, the voting age for men was 21, but the draft age was 18. Only men were drafted, and court decisions at the time linked the right to vote to the obligation to fight for the country. In other words, the courts said that men can vote because men have to fight. So an 18 year old man had to go off and die on a foreign field because he would have the right to vote *three years later*. Unless he was dead, in which case he could only vote in Chicago.

As in so many other cases, *privilege was tied to responsibility*. The privilege to vote was tied to the responsibility to fight in war. Or at least to be subject to the draft.

Let that sink in, and then consider this. Women got the right to vote without the obligation to fight.

So ... who exactly is being oppressed in this deal and who is being privileged?

I am emphatically not trying to defend all the decisions of the past. People do strange, stupid and venal things in every age. And I'm certainly not arguing that women should be drafted. My point is simply that you've heard it all spun from a particular point of view, and there are other points of view. To modern ears, everything is a matter of individual rights. People in other times had other concerns, like family rights, and the obligations that came along with rights. If you try to interpret *their* customs with *our* cultural assumptions, you're bound to get it wrong.

• The marriage strike makes good sense

Marriage is on hard times of late and some people say there is a "marriage strike" going on. Men, they say, have looked at the balance sheet for marriage, and the kinds of inequities I've started to discuss, and have found that the risks outweigh the rewards.

Some of this has to do with the rise of divorce and the fear many men have that they're going to get fleeced in family court. The wife will get the home, the kids, the car, a portion of the man's income, and the kids will be calling some other guy "Dad." Another reason men don't see much point in marriage is something modern women hate to hear. "Why buy the cow when you get the milk for free?" (Just because women hate to hear it doesn't mean men aren't thinking it!)

I've argued that a big part of the driving force behind the traditional approach to marriage is the man's desire for sex. Under the old scheme, if you wanted sex you pretty much had to get married. In today's society, men no longer have to jump through hoops to get sex.

Men don't even have to put as much effort into the pursuit, since women are more aggressive these days. And there's always porn.

Because of all this, one of the big motivations for marriage has evaporated.

Under the old rules, the man was supposed to be the protector and the provider, so it made sense for him to pay for dinner on a date, and to effectively serve as the woman's unpaid bodyguard. That signaled to the woman that he would be able to fulfill his role.

With women working now (sometimes more than men), that arrangement doesn't make as much sense. Men are left wondering why they're supposed to pay, and why if there's trouble they have to physically protect the woman. In earlier generations the men would shout "women and children first" when it came to allocating life rafts. The modern man wonders why.

Many men feel the law no longer protects or respects them, but is stacked against them. Systems designed to prevent sex discrimination, harassment and rape are often incredibly unfair to men. Sometimes the man is guilty until proven innocent — especially on college campuses. And a mere accusation can ruin a man's career.

Settling down and having children used to be a sign of maturity. Men felt as if they were earning respect by growing up and getting married. But maturity isn't valued much now, and fatherhood certainly isn't. Now we worship youth and irresponsibility and we make fun of fathers. Some people treat having children as a crime against the planet.

What would motivate a young man to be a father in today's culture? The father is the goofball who's ridiculed in jokes and commercials and in almost every sitcom.

The job market has changed as well. An average man used to be able to graduate from high school, get a decent job and support a family. That's no longer true in most of the country.

In short, all the traditional calculus for marriage has fallen apart.

Despite all these changes, some legacies of the old system remain. For example, the woman has several choices. She can be a stay-at-home mom. She can have a career. She can do some combination of work and home life.

The man has one choice. He works. Yes, there are stay-at-home dads, but that's pretty rare. The assumption is still that the woman can pursue what fulfills her, but the man has to get a job to support the family.

If the man doesn't have to marry to get sex, and if marriage is no longer the respected path to adulthood, why would a man put up with it — becoming the "success object" of his family, being the *de facto* bread winner, carrying the burden of several lives in addition to his own, and risking the humiliations of a family court that's stacked against him? It's not a very good bargain any more.

There is one other thing that still might push him towards marriage – even with all the modern confusions. What if he wants to have kids? But even there the rules have changed, and it seems too risky to many men. Given the strong possibility of divorce, and the fact that family courts treat men like garbage, why get attached to the little tikes when mom can decide she's unhappy and take them from him – along with the car and the house?

If you're a modern man, you're supposed to initiate and take the risks in a relationship — but the woman can accuse you of sexual harassment or rape and ruin your life. The scales are tilted heavily against men these days. The man is expected to pursue a career so he can support somebody else's lifestyle. That made some sense under the traditional arrangement, where marriage was more stable and included some guarantees, but with easy divorce and a somewhat flaky culture, why take the risk?

It makes perfect sense that a lot of men are concluding that the whole program isn't worth it any more.

Here's the very sad news. They're right. It's not worth it. Under modern assumptions, marriage is bad deal for men. Modern culture has completely ruined the calculus of marriage, and the institution is falling apart as a result.

Still, I think marriage is a great thing. I've been happily married for more than 30 years. But you can't do it the modern way. You have to escape the cultural madness, and you have to find a woman who has escaped it as well.

Marriage simply doesn't fit in the modern world. It's based on a view of the sexes that is not only out of fashion, but *pretty close to illegal.* If you want to be modern, my advice is to forget about marriage. Work out something else that makes you happy. But if you want to marry, my advice is to forget about being modern.

Part 2 — Practical Guidelines

That's enough of a theoretical foundation to start talking about practical issues.

At this point, however, I think it's important to explain why this book was written in the first place.

One of my daughters asked me to have a talk with her boyfriend about being a man. I declined, of course. If he had asked me, that would be one thing, but I'm hardly going to introduce the subject myself. Unless things were to get serious, but .... Anyway, the question got me thinking, "what would I say?" Hence this book.

Up to this point, I think I've been on pretty solid ground. Eggs are expensive, and sperm is cheap, and certain things follow from that logically. From here on out, you should regard my comments as my personal opinions on male-female relationships.

There are some things I would insist on. Men and women are different, and those differences flow from biological reality. I don't think there's any serious argument against that. There are other things I hold to a little more loosely. Maybe it's the 3 percent Neanderthal genes speaking. Or perhaps you should think of what follows as an extended stand-up routine, if that makes you more comfortable. My goal, again, is simply to get another perspective into your head. I'm not proposing legislation or amendments to the Torah.

So then .... If you understand that marriage is a bad deal and that the law and society in general are conspiring to destroy it, but if you think there might be something there for you — under the right circumstances, and with the right woman — then read on. These practical guidelines might help.

• Understand alpha and beta

Remember what was said above about how women need strong genes, protection and provision, but they also need help with the care of the child? These competing needs result in a strange cocktail of desires that can be expressed in terms of alpha and beta traits in men.

Alpha traits are things like leadership, assertiveness, dominance, bravery, and disregard for rules or safety. Beta traits are things like being helpful, being supportive, being reliable and being "nice."

Women are attracted to alpha traits, but they appreciate beta traits. This is why women fall for men with alpha traits but no beta traits — aka "jerks." There's no mystery to it. Women are attracted to those traits because over the last hundred thousand years or so women needed men like that to keep them safe, and they wanted strong genes for their children. That's also why women go all mushy and friendly with "nice guys," but aren't always attracted to them. Nice guys are good to have around, but they're not exciting.

To be a successful husband you have to have both sets of traits, but if you're going to err in one direction, err in the alpha direction.

• Distinguish "good alpha" from "asshole alpha"

If your only reason for pursuing alpha qualities is to be a chick magnet, you don't have to worry about what I'm going to say here. Sometimes being an asshole is a good strategy for attracting women. Or so I'm told. I don't want to be that guy, and if that's your game, put this book down and — as far as I'm concerned — go jump off a bridge.

For the rest of you, just because something is "alpha" doesn't mean it's good. Driving too fast is alpha, but only assholes drive too fast.

You need the alpha traits, but they need to be kept in check. You need to be the warrior, but also the gentleman and the scholar. You need to be the kind of man that elite schools used to try to form young boys into — men who play rugby and then recite poetry in Latin; who volunteer to fight in foreign wars and know what to do when they get there because they memorized parts of the Iliad.

• Women seek to control men, and then they despise the men they can control

The man is the protector for the family. A woman needs to know if a potential mate is tough enough to stand up to life's challenges. She can't put herself in his hands and rely on him only to find out that he's a coward or a weakling. So she watches for signs of weakness. If a man is weak, she'll despise him, dump him, and find somebody else.

In case I haven't made it clear before, let me make sure to point out again that I'm not saying women consciously think these things – any more than men consciously think about the weird things they do. We often don't understand why we do things.

Let me give a personal example to show what I mean.

I was reading a marketing book about persuasion, and how people make choices based on things they're not consciously aware of. Clever marketers exploit those quirks of human nature to sell their products. E.g., a red "buy now" button will get more sales than a yellow one.

While reading that book, I started paying more attention to little things that I do, just to see what kind of weird stuff I'd been doing on autopilot, without thinking – because of some strange animal instinct, perhaps. I noticed that when I'm on an elevator with another person, and that person gets off before me, I move over and stand in his spot.

Why the heck did I do that? Am I a dog that needs to mark territory? (No, I didn't pee on the carpet.)

I don't know if this is unique to me or not, but it made me realize I do a lot of things without thinking about it, or knowing why I do them. And if somebody asked me why, I might come up with a half-baked explanation that has little to do with why I actually do it.

Humans are like that in more ways than they care to admit. We tend to vote for the taller candidate. We tend to interrupt women more than we interrupt men. We do weird stuff, and we don't know why.

So when I say that women test men to see if they're tough, I'm not saying they do it on purpose. They might not even be aware that they're doing it. And in the same way, when men are attracted to women with long hair, they don't understand why. (Long hair – something you can see – may have been a proxy for good health – something you can't see.)

The funny thing is that some of these tests a woman employs to find out if a potential mate is man enough for her are tests of her own making. Some people call them "shit tests," but I don't think that's appropriate. First, I don't like to use that kind of language, but second, it sounds too much like it's a conscious choice.

Maybe I'm wrong about this, but I don't think the woman consciously thinks, "Gee, Joe hasn't stood up to any manhood tests recently. I'd better give him one. What kind of humiliating thing can I try now?"

I suspect it's rather more like this — in the course of being a regular human being, sometimes she will be selfish or nasty or demanding. So will the man, of course. But when a man is a jerk he's wondering "can I get away with this?" and when the woman is a jerk she's also wondering (maybe not consciously) "is he man enough to stop me?"

Pardon my French, but when she's acting like a bitch, a man can either stand up to her, or he can back down. If he backs down, she'll think – maybe consciously, but maybe only subconsciously – "this guy can't even stand up to me, and I only weigh 120 pounds. What a wimp."

If you don't believe me, go to your favorite search engine and type "women hate harmless men."

Again, I think it's best not to think of these things as calculated tests. Women probably don't plan them, and they might not even know they're doing them. They'll just observe and start to form the idea that this guy is not for her. Then she'll despise him for it — even if she doesn't recognize that's what she's doing.

Along these lines, I have a personal theory that I submit for your consideration. I've observed that in older married couples, the woman often develops the habit of belittling the husband, criticizing him publicly, and sometimes even treating him like a child. I suspect some of this has to do with the fact that older men have less testosterone, and they're more likely to act like a wimp. They choose to go along to get along, because it's just too much work to fight. As the years go by, this takes a toll on the woman's opinion of her husband.

Maybe that's complete baloney. It's just a little theory I have.

• The man is the head of the home

Yes, yes, I know how that sounds to modern ears. Your brain immediately jumps to "but, but, but" – if you haven't already simply closed down your mind and decided not to pay attention any more.

I also know that it sounds a little odd after I've been laboring the point that women are more important to the species. If women are more important, why aren't they the head of the home?

Well, who says "more important" means "head"?

Women are "more important" in the sense I have outlined in this book, namely that society needs women more than it needs men because women are more vital to humanity's survival. That has very little to do with being the head of the home.

And no, I'm not going to explain what "head of the home" means right here for the simple reason that this whole book is about being the head of the home. I could just as well have titled this book "What you need to know to be the head of your home."

At this point, all I want to say is that the man *is* the head of the home. I'm not saying that he should be, or that he should try to be, or that the wife should let him be. No. He is the head of the home whether anybody likes that fact or not. Everything I'm saying here is part of the explanation, but to give a two-second overview, (1) by his very nature the man is more suited to being the leader, and (2) women know that, which is why they despise men they can control.

At this point someone might raise the objection that while these things may be true of men and women *in general*, they're not necessarily true of every man and every woman. There may be exceptions.

Well … yes. I'm not Moses and this isn't the Torah. I'm not trying to lay down absolute rules. The realities of life can be pretty strange at times, and general rules aren't always applicable in all situations. If people want to have their own arrangements, that's their business and none of mine.

Please remember that the point of this little book is to give you another perspective on these issues. I'm trying to give you another way to look at things, not to lay down absolute moral principles that have to be followed in every circumstance.

So then, given that caveat, let me say this. As a general rule, a man is either going to act like the head of the home or he's going to have a frustrated, unhappy, confused wife. *Of course* there may be exceptions. But that's the way it is most of the time.

• If you follow this advice you'll be called a sexist

The prevailing attitude in the culture today is very different from the attitudes expressed in this little book, which will undoubtedly be called sexist by the politically correct.

Good.

The modern fantasy about the sexes, and about love and marriage in general, is clearly, demonstrably, objectively wrong, so why would you want to follow it? Why would you want the praise and acceptance of people who have bought into a crazy, self-destructive, counter-factual viewpoint?

In my opinion, if you're not called a sexist from time to time, you're doing something wrong. However, it's important to make a distinction between different kinds of "sexist."

To some, it's sexist to suggest that men and women are different. You shouldn't care about being called that kind of sexist for the simple reason that men and women actually are different. If people can't deal with reality, that's their problem.

Another version of sexism is to say that one sex is better than the other.

You can understand "better" in at least a couple ways – in terms of value or in terms of function. In terms of value, a man is better than a chicken, but in terms of function, a chicken is better than a man – for laying eggs, for example. Women and men are equally valuable, but they clearly have different capabilities, and men (on average) are better at some things than women (on average) and vice versa.

A general statement that one sex is "better" than the other is just nonsense. It depends entirely on what you mean. Your average man is a better mechanic, but your average woman is a better nurse. That doesn't mean a woman can't be a great mechanic.

You might also be accused of sexism for saying that one sex is more important than the other, and on that point — once again — you should be happy to be called a sexist because women are far more important than men — at least as far as the survival of the species is concerned. A society can lose lots of men and keep going. It can't lose lots of women.

The bottom line is this: don't let "sexism" scare you. If somebody calls you a sexist, thank him and buy him a drink.

• Don't create a "man cave"

Being the head of the home doesn't mean you have a "man cave." In fact — this might just be my own prejudice, but this whole book is about my own prejudices, so I might as well say it — I dislike the whole concept of the man cave.

"Man cave" is one of those phrases that makes me cringe. For two reasons. First, it infantilizes men. "There you go, little boy. Go play Neanderthal in your cave. Yes, you can take your toys with you. Just be ready to come when I call." Second, it implies that the "man's domain" is somewhere else – an unimportant part of the house, like the garage or the basement. The rest of the house belongs to the wife.

That is a fundamentally flawed view. The house is the man's castle. The whole thing.

That doesn't mean he shouldn't accommodate his wife and children or try to make them happy. Rather, to the contrary. It also doesn't mean, for example, that the wife can't have a special place for her hobbies, or that the kids can't decorate their rooms the way they want. Since it is the man's house, and since he is a servant-leader (more on that below), he respects the needs and desires of the people under his care.

The man might need a workshop, or a home office, or an exercise room, where he does specific things. But that is a different thing from a "man cave." The point of a "man cave" — or, at least this is how it has always seemed to me — is to be a special place where the man feels comfortable and at home.

No, no, no! The man should feel comfortable in his entire house. Any woman who tries to make the house uninviting to the man (except in the "man cave") is not a good wife, and any man who has to retreat to a "man cave" to feel comfortable in his house is not a good man. The man should be comfortable in the kitchen, in his daughter's pink bedroom and in the workshop — because he knows that these are essential parts of the home.

• Be Captain Picard

The husband is the captain and the wife is the first officer. As Captain, the man needs to set an example.

Think of the Star Trek movie "Generations," where we see Captain Kirk and Captain Picard side by side. I happen to like William Shatner a lot. I loved Star Trek growing up, and I think Mr. Shatner is a very talented and interesting person. But when I see him next to Patrick Stewart I have to think, "Bill, you're Captain of the Enterprise. Hit the gym!"

As a man, you have to outrank your wife. I realize that's an odd thing to say, but I mean it in two ways. In the sense that the man is the head of the home, he outranks her because he is the captain and she's the first officer. But there's another sense of "rank," and that is the respective ranks of the man and the woman in the sexual marketplace.

"Sex rank" is a complicated concept that other people can explain better than I can, but the basic idea is that certain characteristics give men and women more pull in the dating game. Remember, this is an unapologetically sexist book that does not pretend that men and women are equal. The factors that give a man a better sex rank are different from the factors that give a woman a better sex rank because men and women are attracted to different things.

For example, being tall is better for a man than it is for a woman. Having long hair is better for a woman than it is for a man. Carrying an extra 20 pounds isn't good for anybody, but it's worse for a woman than it is for a man. (Go ahead and call me sexist. I'll just say "thank you.")

I would like to stress that none of these things are absolutes. It's not as if a short man or a woman with short hair can't have a lot of game. These are generalizations.

A woman ranks higher when she is young, attractive and fun. A man ranks higher when he's a leader, confident (and maybe a little arrogant), and successful. There's more to it, but that's good enough for now.

It may seem like a difficult task to outrank your wife, especially if you're marrying a good-looking 23 year old, because they have a really high sex rank. The good thing for you is that a man's sex rank isn't as influenced by a role of the biological dice. That is, it doesn't depend so much on your looks. You can increase your sex rank by what you do.

Be decisive. Be successful. Be fit. Dress well. Know how to fix a car and replace a faucet. In short, be a man. (Or, if you need an example, be Captain Picard.)

You need to be attractive to other women. This will fire your wife's competitive instincts and she will try to keep up.

This may sound a little confusing. Why would you want to be attractive to women other than your wife? I've already said I don't like the player culture, and I'm trying to suggest how to make a marriage work. In that situation, doesn't the man only need to appeal to his wife?

A man who only tries to please his wife and doesn't care what other women think is displaying a misguided sort of piety. It sounds very noble — "I only care what my wife thinks" — but it's not a good idea. For one thing, you don't always know what your wife likes, and frankly, she might not either. Attraction is a mysterious thing.

You need to be the kind of a man who is attractive to other women in general in order to be attractive to any woman in particular.

You have to maintain a balance between two seemingly contradictory things. First, you need to let her know that you are a faithful, reliable man who would never hurt her, leave her or betray her. Second, she should know that other women notice when you walk into the room.

Be a man that other women find attractive. That's not an invitation to cheat or flirt (more on that later), but it's a goal you have to keep in mind.

• Learn the difference between "flirting" and "generating attraction"

You need to know how to be attractive to women — or, in other words, how to be the kind of man that women find attractive.

At a very basic level, every woman is attracted to every man and vice versa. (Yes, I'm speaking in generalities that wouldn't apply in all cases, e.g., to someone with same-sex attraction.)

We're attracted to one another because we're men and women, and that's how things work. However, we have to be selective in where and on whom we expend our time and energy, and that's where attraction comes in.

Think of it this way. Let's say the human population has two groups of men. Group A men are attracted to sickly, diseased women, while Group B men are attracted to healthy, vigorous women. It stands to reason that after a few generations, Group A will be gone, because they've invested their genes in women who don't have much chance of raising healthy offspring. The men in Group A are pursuing a genetic dead end.

Following that same sort of logic, in the natural course of things the people whose attractions cause them to invest in success will tend to dominate the population. That would seem to imply that the men who are attracted to healthy women who can bear children will pass on their genes.

It gets more confusing when you talk about women's attraction because women have different sorts of needs. A man "invests" his genes and he's mostly done. Women have a longer process. If they invest in alpha types, they'll pass on genes for strong, manly offspring, but the alpha guy might abandon them, and then they'll be left with a newborn on their hip trying to fight off the rhinoceros all by themselves. No matter how alpha that newborn is, he's not going to help much against the rhinoceros.

On the other hand, if they invest in beta types, they'll have somebody there to help them raise the child and change the diapers, but he'll try to negotiate with the rhinoceros.

Some people say this leads women to want the alpha's genes but the beta's commitment, and … there are some not very nice implications of that.

The key point to keep in mind is that women have mixed desires in a mate. *They say* they are attracted to kind, thoughtful, reliable, domestic men, but they swoon over millionaires, actors, politicians and rock stars, who are neither kind, thoughtful nor reliable.

I recently learned that my list (millionaires, actors, etc.) is not quite right. Google engineers looked at search results to find out what women are attracted to. The list is … a little disturbing, and rather funny. The top five are vampire, werewolf, billionaire, surgeon, and pirate.

This is, of course, a distorted look at what women want, just as a man's search history would be a distorted look at what he really wants. No matter how often men fantasize about things, I doubt they want those things in the real world.

The truth is that women want alpha and beta traits, but perhaps at different times. (Some studies allegedly show that a woman's sexual preferences change with her menstrual cycle.) One way to understand this is to assume that women wish the alphas they are attracted to also had beta qualities. They aren't often *attracted to* beta qualities, but they appreciate them. The alpha qualities are exciting while the beta qualities are comforting.

So those are your marching orders. You need a mix of alpha and beta. Be an alpha who generates attraction, but also be a beta who generates comfort. But don't confuse what women *say* they are attracted to with what they are actually attracted to. They will say they're attracted to betas, and if you follow that advice you'll become a weenie your girl will grow to despise.

However, while you want to be a man who generates attraction, you do not want to arouse emotions in a woman that you can't rightly fulfill. It's perfectly fine for the other women in the room to think you're attractive. It's not fine for you to lead them on, or to imply that you'll do something you're not going to do. That's being a tease. Flirting may be "alpha," but it's asshole alpha, and it's not manly. Or at least not gentlemanly.

Become a man women are attracted to, but don't flirt — unless, of course, you mean it. Then dress the part and do your best.

Also remember that women want gestures of investment, commitment and love, but they only want them from men to whom they are attracted. To be a good husband you need to do the things that make you attractive to women (i.e., be successful, be a leader, be assertive, have goals, stay in shape) and then show those gestures of love and commitment to your wife. Keep the attraction going and the gestures of investment will be appreciated.

• You need to have an agenda and a purpose

Women want to hitch their wagon to a man who is going someplace. This is part of the reason why rock stars and actors and millionaires have no trouble picking up chicks, even if they're old and ugly, or even if they're young dreamers with few prospects.

You're almost certainly not going to be a rock star or a successful actor. But you can be a man with a mission. You can be a man of passion. You can have things in life that you enjoy.

It doesn't matter too much what your mission or your passion is, but you have to have one, and you have to pursue it.

Women may complain about a man who spends too much time fixing his classic car, but they'd much rather have him than a man who spends all his time on the couch in front of the idiot box.

• You need to be a servant leader

Most of the advice you'll get on the concept of being a servant leader emphasizes the servant part. Some people will tell you that the husband as "servant leader" means he's supposed to "serve" his wife – that he leads by serving. Don't listen to those people, not even with one ear.

The concept of a servant leader comes from the Gospels. When Jesus spoke about servant leaders, he was speaking to a culture that emphasized the "leader" part too much, and he wanted to emphasize more of the "servant" part.

Today — at least in terms of male-female relationships — we have the opposite problem. Everyone will tell a man he has to serve his wife, but precious few will tell him he has to lead her. Some will try to rescue this by saying that the way a man leads is to serve, but that's nonsense for the castrati.

Jesus is supposed to be the prototypical servant leader. So I ask you — did he ask the apostles' permission to do things? Did he make sure he checked with them before he overturned the tables of the money-lenders, or rode into Jerusalem? Did he ask their opinion before raising Lazarus from the dead?

Of course not. "Servant leader" means that you lead for the benefit of the people you are leading. It absolutely does not mean that you get their permission or always do things their way. That's sissy talk from men who have abandoned both their masculinity and their sense.

• Men are called to sacrifice

As I've mentioned many times, a culture can lose most of its men and still survive. It can't lose many of its women or children. The lesson you need to take from this is that men are disposable.

Warren Farrell has a very good book called *The Myth of Male Power* that you might want to read. He makes some good points, but in my opinion he's too infected with the myth of equality and he gets a few things wrong as a result.

He would characterize the idea of the disposable man as a "stage 1" situation. Men were disposable back when the culture was in "survival mode," but we've moved past that now.

I agree with Farrell that we're no longer in survival mode (or at least not to the same degree), but I disagree that we can move past the old rules because we live in generally peaceful countries and have microwave ovens and antibiotics. I think there's something called human nature, and that we're pretty much stuck with it — at least for the next 10,000 years or so.

Men have been groomed and trained over many thousands of years to be the warriors. Women have been groomed and trained over many thousands of years to be the nurturers. This grooming isn't just cultural. It's in our genes. That's not going to change because somebody has invented a mechanical dishwasher and the internal combustion engine.

Part of becoming a man is learning that you are disposable. When the ship is going down, women and children get the spots in the life boats. When the Hun is racing across the plain, your body stands between their axe and your village. When the child has fallen into a well, you go down there to get him out. We all want you to survive the ordeal, but ... when it comes right down to it ....

Is this fair? Of course not. Fairness is sissy talk.

It's also not fair that when a country needs sailors, they simply grab young men off the dock and stick them on the ship. Or that when they need soldiers, they put a rifle in a young man's hands and tell him to fight or get shot as a deserter.

That's the way things used to be – and still are, in some places – and there was a reason for it that you ought to know by now.

It's also not fair that women die in childbirth. It's not fair that women are so comparatively small and weak that when you die failing to keep the Hun from getting through the gate she doesn't have a prayer of defending herself. She gets raped and hauled off to bear little Hun babies. If she's lucky.

Life is not fair. Or, as the Man in Black said in "The Princess Bride," "Life is pain, Highness. Anyone who says differently is selling something."

At this point I imagine there are two voices struggling in your brain. One is the voice of modern civilization telling you we need to get past all that. We need a new humanity. We need a utopian future where men and women can be equal and we aren't slaves to these barbaric impulses.

The other voice is your inner warrior, whose heart has been stirred. He hears the sound of approaching hoof beats and he says, "Bring me my broadsword."

All you need to know is this: it's the second guy who gets the chicks.

• Boys need to play rough sports and fight

It should be obvious by now why boys play rough, and why it's in society's interests to promote that kind of behavior.

If someone were to ask you why boys' lacrosse has one set of rules and girls' lacrosse has another, you should know the answer. Boys are being trained to ignore pain and suffering, to put the group first, to sacrifice themselves for the cause, and to seek glory in victory. In short, boys are socialized into that mindset because it's in society's best interests to have tough boys who can be soldiers. A nation of weenies has no hope of stopping the Hun.

We have no such interest with women. We don't want women fighting the Hun because, on the one hand, they're smaller and weaker and won't make as effective soldiers as the guys, but more importantly, because eggs are too expensive to be tossing them away like that.

Now you know why Title IX is stupid beyond words.

The world is a fairly safe place for most of us these days, and you probably won't have to defend your village against the Hun. But you need to know how to fight anyway. Few things are more pathetic than the guy who's afraid to fight. You need to get over that fear. Take boxing lessons. Take martial arts in a studio where you can spar. Get a bloody nose a few times. You'll quickly learn that a little bit of pain is no big deal, and a man who is afraid of pain is no man at all.

You also need to learn some basic fighting techniques. You don't need to be Jackie Chan, but you don't want to be that guy who just flails around and doesn't know what he's doing. Learn the basics of punching and blocking, takedowns, submission holds and ground fighting.

Along these lines, make sure to regularly mock the idea of the female warrior that the movies are trying to promote these days. It's complete lunacy.

Soldiers are big, strong, tough guys who carry lots of gear and have to do strenuous, hard things.

I like Lucy Liu. She's a very interesting character in Elementary. But the Lucy Liu in Charlie's Angels is just silly. If she tried to punch your average soldier, all she'd do is break her wrist.

War is a man's enterprise for many reasons. It's not only because sperm is cheap. It's also because men are larger, stronger and more aggressive. They are also more able to push their feelings aside and go do the horrible things that war requires.

There might be one woman in ten thousand who can actually pass the physical requirements to be a soldier, and I don't intend to diminish their service (although I think it's misguided from a sociological perspective). But why should we kid ourselves? War is a man's game.

• Don't defend yourself (if you're not in physical danger)

The man I'm suggesting you emulate has swagger. He's assertive, bold and cocky. He can defend himself in a fight. But because he's confident, he can also be polite and act like a gentleman. He's an iron fist in a velvet glove.

You're not an iron fist if you're always defending yourself or making excuses. Defending yourself is usually self-defeating and makes you look like a wimp. If you were wrong about something, be a man and admit you were wrong.

> Boss: This report is late.
>
> Defensive approach: I'm sorry, I was so busy with the Philips case that I couldn't get this done ....

The message you're sending is that you can't manage your time, you're inefficient, and now you're whining about it. The boss can't trust you to do anything.

> Boss: This report is late.
>
> Proper approach: I had to put more important projects first. I'll have it for you this afternoon.

With this approach you were bold and decisive. You figured that something else was more important, so you did that one first, but you'll still fulfill your obligation.

• Do apologize when you're wrong

If you missed your deadline because you were lazy, or inefficient, or just forgot, then you can't claim to have been pursuing a higher purpose.

> Boss: This report is late.
>
> Apologize: That was my mistake. I'll have it for you this afternoon.

In this case you take responsibility for your actions and you resolve to fix things.

If you walk into your boss' office and say, "I screwed up. This is what I did, and this is how I'm going to fix it," your boss will think better of you. Everybody makes mistakes, but in this situation your boss isn't thinking, "I need to keep an eye on that one. He's always hiding his mistakes from me." Rather, you took ownership of your mistake and you fixed it, *without making your boss have to do anything.*

That's behaving like a man.

You have to do this same thing with your girl. Admit when you're wrong. Don't get defensive. Don't let it turn into a blame fest. Don't put up with a bunch of crap. Just admit that you were wrong, do what you can to fix it, and move on.

• Make statements, don't ask questions

This is a general rule, and it falls under the broader heading of being a confident guy. There are times when you have to ask questions, but when you have a choice between asking a question and making a statement, make a statement. It's the more socially dominant way to behave. That is, it's acting like a man.

I know, I know. You've been trained to think that "dominant" is a bad word. You should be humble and meek. Unassuming.

Forget all that.

Yes, of course you should be humble about certain things. You should be humble about all the amazing benefits you've received from the sacrifices of other people. You should be humble and modest in victory. You should be humble before your parents and elders. You should have people in your life (i.e., male friends) that play the part of the court jester to put you in your place from time to time.

But in your interactions with most of the world you are confident, bold and assertive.

• Educate yourself

You want to cultivate the ability to keep people interested in what you're saying, which usually means two things. First, keep your mind active and know interesting things to talk about. Second, know when to shut up. Not everyone is interested in all the details of your favorite TV show.

Learn about interesting things. Graduating from school is not the end of your education — it's just the beginning. There are a million interesting things out there, and you should be passionate about finding them out — or at least some of them.

The problem with knowing too much is that you can bore people. You need to learn the signs and learn to move on. People tend to give clues to what they're thinking. If you don't pick up on them naturally, study them.

For example, if a woman gives short, perfunctory responses to what you say, or if she's slouching and leaning, she's probably bored. If a man folds his arms, he's sheltering himself against what you're saying. He doesn't like it.

Be the guy people want to listen to. Have something interesting to say, but be a little mysterious by holding some things back, and know when to quit.

• Dress well

Next time you're walking around in the city, pay attention to the other men. You'll look at one man, and something about him will shout "he looks like somebody," and then you'll look at another guy, and the universe will quietly mutter, "what a schlub."

A very small part of this is the genetic lottery. You can't make yourself taller, and it costs a lot to fix that ugly nose. But you can stand up straight, you can hold your shoulders back, and you can dress like a man.

You may be tempted to think that it's "putting on airs," or pretending.

Okay, fine. Next time, go outside dirty and naked, with uncut hair and untrimmed finger nails. And make sure that you go poop in the woods with no toilet paper.

There, now you're not pretending any more. Do you feel better?

Civilization is about rising above the brutish realities of life. We wash ourselves, or wear cologne if we have to. We clothe our bodies, and not merely for warmth.

Dressing well shows respect for yourself and for other people. And you'll find that if you dress well, people will treat you well.

I wear a hat, because I have a fair complexion, and I need to keep the sun off my face. I find that the more I exercise, and watch my weight, the more attractive women compliment me on my hat.

• Exercise

Another part of not being a schlub is keeping yourself fit. As you age you will tend to slow down and put on weight. You need to resist that by watching your diet and keeping active. The discipline of foregoing that second cup of corn flakes will help you in ways you can hardly imagine, as will the discipline of forcing yourself out of bed to go for a jog in the cold.

One good piece of advice for men: buy a tuxedo when you're 30, and stay that size.

• Learn personal finance

You need to be a competent manager of your resources.

Women want a provider — not only for themselves, but for their offspring. They don't want to invest all that time and effort to raise a kid who's going to starve because you can't gather enough in the harvest to keep food on the table all winter.

Learn the basics of how to manage money, and make that a part of your life. There's tons of information online, but the general rules are simple. Stay out of debt. Invest in your retirement. Live below your means.

• Get a toolbox and learn to fix things

There was a time when cars were simple enough that your average guy could do most of the needful repairs. Cars have become a lot more complicated these days and it's hard for the weekend mechanic to keep up. Still, you should have a basic understanding of how cars work, and you should be able to change the oil, change a tire, jump start a car and deal with routine maintenance.

The same is true in your house. Learn basic electronics and plumbing, how to hang curtain rods, simple woodworking, and so on. Women appreciate a man who can fix things.

In the mixed up modern world, it's reasonable to expect you to change the tire or fix the leaky toilet, but it's unreasonable to expect her to make lunch while you're doing it. It's reasonable to expect you to mow the lawn, but unreasonable to expect her to sew the button on your jacket. It's reasonable when somebody is moving that you will volunteer and move the heavy stuff. It's unreasonable to expect the women to provide drinks and food. (In fact, you'll probably have to spring for carry out.)

Be unreasonable.

• You need to be sensitive and caring, but from a position of strength

Women are attracted to alpha jerks, but they appreciate sensitive, nice guys. You don't want to be either one. Or, rather, you want to be the best of both.

The jerk is completely alpha and grabs the woman's attention and attraction. The nice guy is completely beta. He dries her tears and hopes for some love, but she treats him like a friend. Isn't that precious.

Don't be either guy — the jerk who attracts women only to break their heart, or the hanger-on who can never get out of the friend zone.

You want to be like a knight of the round table. Tough, bold, decisive and commanding, but gentle, caring and considerate.

• Help with the laundry, but only sometimes

You should be willing to help your wife with the laundry or the dishes when she's overwhelmed, or just to give her a break, and you clearly need to share the chores if you're both working, but the modern world has gone a little too far in the "share the housework" direction.

Generally speaking, "keeping house" is the woman's task and "taming the wilderness" is the man's task. A few decades ago "taming the wilderness" became "climbing the company ladder" because of the lack of wilderness to be tamed.

I think a mother should stay home with the children (at least when they're very young), and during that phase of life the traditional roles are easier to follow. Later, if husband and wife are both working, it gets a little more complicated and requires some give and take. There's nothing wrong with that, just don't fall for the cultural sickness that thinks it's wrong to have sex-specific tasks. Sex-appropriate tasks are a good thing because men and women are, in fact, different.

Generally speaking, her domain is the kitchen and the nursery, yours is the workshop and the garage. I know that sounds sexist and old fashioned. Good.

• Be considerate of her emotional state

Women are more emotional than men. I don't know if women *feel* or *experience* emotion more or less than men, and I don't know how you would test that idea in any event. But women express things in emotional terms more often than men do.

There are a lot of reasons for that. One is that it makes people more likely to want to protect them, and women need protection for all the reasons we've discussed. On the other side of the ledger, it's good that men are less emotional because you generally don't get to take a break to sit down and cry for a while on the battlefield.

"Can we charge later, Captain? I need a few minutes."

I know that some women take offense at the idea that they're more emotional, and many don't feel that they need to be protected. Also, "women are more emotional" is a generalization, and isn't true in every case. Some women are tough and some men are wimps.

Part of the modern delusion is to think that any exception destroys the general principle. The occasional Joan of Arc does not change the general fact that men are larger, stronger, less emotionally attached, and better suited to combat, while women are designed to be mothers, and therefore need the protection of their mates and their clan.

It's true that things are different in the modern world and women don't need the same sort of protection that they used to need. The Hun and the saber tooth tiger rarely visit the suburbs. But we're still the same creatures we were back when they did. Men are still much larger and stronger than women and still have the same instincts they did when the men of the clan had to grab a long stick and fight off a bear.

Just for fun, let's assume that the modern world has eliminated the need for men to protect women. Even in that case, we still have the instincts, prejudices and feelings we've developed over thousands of years. Our emotions and attractions adapted to a different world. It's simply part of our nature for men to protect women, and it's part of a woman's nature to expect and appreciate that.

It's important to remember why. Aside from being smaller and weaker than the men in the clan, the women only have a few shots at passing on their genes, and each one of those attempts puts them at serious risk. The women are going to be the primary caregivers for a mostly helpless little guy clinging to their hips. They need help with that task. They need the rest of the clan to instinctively want to protect them. Because of that, it makes perfect sense for women to develop traits that encourage a protective attitude in others.

If you have a few moments, you might want to watch a Youtube video called Neoteny by girlwriteswhat.

I don't know if she has everything exactly right, but it provides an interesting perspective on this issue.

The bottom line is this — women are different from men. Women developed under a different set of rules. One difference is that women are (in general, not in every case) more emotional. There's good and bad to that, but you're going to have to deal with it whether you like it or not.

• Speak to men and women differently

Frequently you'll hear somebody moan, complain, or make excuses, and as a responsible man with a spine and a brain your inner reaction will be "get over it you little cry baby." That is precisely how you should treat most men in many situations. If they act like wimps, call them out as wimps. A man will either take your criticism to heart and change, or he'll tell you you're an ass. Either way, you've aired your complaint and everything is fine.

Unfortunately, we live in an age where everything has to be qualified and explained. *Obviously* there are times when men need sympathy and encouragement. Remember, I'm not Moses, and I'm not writing laws. I'm simply trying unbend a little of the bent attitudes that have infected our society, and by being a little outrageous I'm trying to help you give yourself permission to believe and say the things you (probably) already believe.

Gosh I hate that sort of back-pedaling crap. But it's necessary.

In any event, the same approach doesn't work with women. Women have a need to be understood that simply confounds and confuses most men. To some degree this is because men emphasize the outer life and women emphasize the inner life. Or, in other words, "what you do" matters more to men, "how you feel" matters more to women. That's an over-simplification, but it's a helpful over-simplification.

If you say "your shirt looks stupid" to a man, he'll think you're talking about the shirt. If you say "your blouse looks awful" to a woman, she may think you're talking about her blouse, but she'll also think you're insulting her sense of taste in general, and she'll almost certainly think you're mad at her, and she'll wonder what she did to earn it. Then, when she concludes she didn't do anything wrong, she'll decide it's all your fault and you're being an ass. The blouse hardly comes into it at all.

You have to express your dislike for the blouse in the form of a back-handed compliment. "I think your pink blouse looks better with that skirt." Don't worry, she'll get the point that you don't like the blouse she's wearing, but she'll also get that you remembered her other blouse, that you noticed it looked good on her, and she'll realize it actually does look better with this skirt. Assuming you have any sense of taste.

All this requires men to do a lot of mental work they're not used to doing. You can't bring the habits you learned among the guys into a marriage and expect it to work. You need to adjust.

When you see your girlfriend or wife looking good in some outfit, that's enough for you. You're happy. You don't feel the need to *say* anything about it, and you certainly don't feel the need to make some sort of record in your mental database.

That's not going to be good enough when dealing with a woman. You need to notice that she looks good. You need to mention it. You need to remember it so that when she wears the dorky outfit you can make the appropriate comment.

I know you're thinking "why can't women just ...."

Stop. That's a madman speaking. Suppress that voice until it dies a lonely death.

One of the essential stupidities of modern life is the idea that men and women are interchangeable and can start acting like one another. Women are simply not going to start thinking or reacting the way you want them to think or react. You have to adapt.

• Learn how to speak to women

Everybody needs affirmation, but men and women get their affirmation in different ways. For some people, knowing that they've done something well is all the praise they need. For others, praise actually motivates them.

You mow your lawn because you don't want the neighbor to look at your scraggly, overgrown lawn and think you're a lazy bum. Or maybe just because you value excellence and want a good-looking yard. The fact that someone might praise you for the condition of your lawn is nice, but it's not the thing that motivates you.

I suspect, but I don't really know, that women are more motivated by praise than men are, and I suspect this is part of the reason why everybody gets a ribbon or a trophy in sports these days. Women have become much more involved in organized sports, and the female perspective ("motivate through praise") has become more dominant in our society in general.

I could be completely wrong about that – it's just a theory. Think about it yourself for a while and see if it makes sense. In any event, your takeaway is to pay attention to how your sweetheart responds to praise and to criticism. You'll have a tendency to "fire and forget." E.g., "I told you that I don't like peas cooked this much."

You will think that you said what you wanted, and if she wants to please you she should remember and do it that way. Simple, right?

Sorry, the world isn't like that. You are going to have to reach deep into weird parts of your brain to figure out how to say things. If you were in a house full of guys, you would say, "Hey, next time cook the peas about half this long," and that would be that. If that didn't work, the next time you'd say it a little more forcefully.

That's not going to work with a woman. You might need to try something like, "Thanks for cooking peas. I like peas," and then just *hope* that she says something like, "Is this the way you like them?" Then you can say something like, "These are good, but I like them even better if they're cooked a little less."

Now she feels appreciated. Not only did she cook something that you like, but now she knows how to do it better next time.

When you're dealing with a woman you are dealing with an alien creature. She does not react the way you react.

However, remember to be honest in your speech and actions. Your praise and compliments matter because they're rare and because you speak the truth. You should regularly say the polite, nice things that oil social relationships and make life run more smoothly, but "you look nice today" is meaningless if you say it every day.

• Women expect other people to affirm their feelings

This gets back to the whole "don't try to solve my problem" thing. If you haven't seen it yet, this is brilliantly illustrated in "it's not about the nail" on Youtube.

The story goes basically like this. Guys talk about a problem so they can solve it. Women talk about a problem to solve the problem, but also so they can empathize with one another. In some cases, anyway. When they complain about the dishwasher, they really do want you to fix the dishwasher. But when the wife comes home and complains about such and so in the office, the man immediately thinks, "Ah, she is asking me to solve this for her, just like I fixed the dishwasher last week."

If you try to "solve the problem" with some sage advice, what she'll hear is "he thinks I'm so stupid that I couldn't come up with any of those lame ideas by myself." Your attempt to solve the problem makes her mad. What you were supposed to do was listen and empathize.

Consider the following two examples.

A man generally would not say "you don't take me seriously" to other men because he knows he'd be insulting himself. By saying that he would be placing himself in a subservient position, and the other men would be happy to confirm him there. "You're right. We don't take you seriously." The man might as well put a "kick me" sign on his back.

There's a different dynamic going on with women. If a woman were to say to other women, "you don't take me seriously," she would say it as an insult *to the other women* because they have failed to recognize and affirm her feelings. Women have a completely different perspective on "being vulnerable."

I know, I know. We've all been told that men need to quit the macho stuff, show their feelings and learn to be more vulnerable. Why are we doing this? Are we going to start telling male robins that they have to start helping with the duty of building the nest? Isn't it possible that men and women are simply different?

Should men learn to "be more vulnerable" in some situations? I don't know, maybe in some limited cases. But we have to be willing to recognize what men are for. They're supposed to stand in the gate and stop the marauding Hun. They're not supposed to stand there and be vulnerable.

Being non-vulnerable is part of who a man is, and men are that way by nature, reinforced by socialization and by the fact that women appreciate men like that. That's not all going to change because some sensitive guy in a sweater says it's a good idea.

Men are more direct, and that's what they expect in others. Unfortunately, women are not always as direct. Sometimes they don't tell you exactly what they want – e.g., when something is broken and needs to be fixed.

"Does it feel chilly in here?" means "get up and close the window." If you just say "no" and go on reading the paper, she'll think you're an uncaring oaf. If you get up and close the window for her, you might get some "nice guy" points, but don't do that too much. (Remember alpha and beta.)

You might try something like, "No. Maybe you should put on a sweater," which recognizes that she's cold (you empathized! Hurray!), but also treats her like an adult who can take care of her own problems.

The most brilliant reply I've ever heard was a man who said, "I don't know. Why don't you call some of your friends and ask them." But I don't recommend that.

• Control your eyes

You need to learn the discipline to keep your eyes where they belong. It's simply childish to be gazing longingly at something you have no right to.

Imagine you're at a birthday dinner and there are two cakes. One is a very fancy cake made by a pastry chef, especially for the birthday boy. The other is an ordinary sheet cake for everyone else. Now imagine the guests are all looking longingly at the special cake. Maybe even licking their lips.

That's how inappropriate it is for you to be looking longingly at other women. It's childish.

There's nothing wrong with appreciating a woman's beauty in the right time and place. In fact, it may be wrong not to. Think of what Alice Walker says in "The Color Purple": "I think it pisses God off if you walk by the color purple in a field somewhere and don't notice it."

Women are incredibly beautiful. But there's a right way and a wrong way to appreciate that fact.

One thing that may be helpful is to think about the difference in how you react to Grace Kelly and how you react to Sharon Stone. (If you don't know who Grace Kelly is, look her up on IMDB and rent a movie or two.) Physically the two women are very similar, but Grace Kelly looks and acts like a lady, while Sharon Stone does not (or at least often she does not). Your sweetheart probably doesn't mind that you think Grace Kelly is attractive, but she won't like it if you think Sharon Stone is attractive. The difference isn't in their physical attributes, it's in *what they're trying to attract.*

The grand deception about sex and sex roles that I've been talking about has influenced women as well as men. In many ways it's affected women more. They've been taught that it's okay to walk around in public looking like a hooker, and you're affirming them when you follow them with your eyes.

Be the man, be a leader and set a better example. When a woman dresses well and looks classy, compliment her on it. But don't give any attention to the women who dress like street walkers. Treat them the way they deserve — as someone who is embarrassing herself and is too clueless to realize it.

• No porn

How would you like it if your girlfriend spent some time every day getting aroused reading stories of rich, successful men? (Or, if we follow the findings of the Google engineers, vampires, werewolves, billionaires, surgeons and pirates.)

That may be a close approximation to how she feels about you looking at porn.

Please don't get me wrong. I am absolutely not saying that all your behavior should be governed by what a woman likes or doesn't like. That is the path to castration — to the total obliteration of your manhood. You will become a quivering jelly of a man, and she will despise you. There are times when you have to do things she does not like.

On porn, however, she's right.

There are lots of reasons why porn is bad for you. Some of the more obvious ones are ...

- women aren't like that
- most women don't like the things porn stars do
- you're creating a very false image of sex in your mind that will mess up your real sex life
- you're supporting an industry that abuses people

- porn is about free, uncommitted sex with no consequences, and that is (1) unrealistic, and (2) the exact opposite of the moral stance you should be taking in life.

There's another reason you may not have considered, and it only applies after you're married.

If you and your wife are mad at each other, you're not going to have sex. But you want to have sex, so you want to resolve the conflict — whatever it is. Therefore your sex drive encourages you to have the talk, apologize, confront her if she did something wrong, or do whatever it is you have to do to get past the dispute and get back to bed.

If you're bleeding off your sexual tension with porn, you lose that incentive to set things right with your wife. That becomes a death spiral.

If your wife is your only legitimate outlet for sex (as she should be), you're going to be motivated to maintain a healthy relationship.

• No sex outside of marriage

Your sex drive is a very powerful part of you. It's like a wild stallion. It's also about as useful as a wild stallion. That is, it's not useful at all. It won't plow, and you can't ride it.

You may be thinking, "yeah, but I'd rather be a wild stallion. I don't want a saddle or a yoke." Or, as Bill Maher put it recently, "Married men live longer than unmarried men. And an indoor cat ...."

You're not faced with a choice between being a wild stallion or being an indoor cat. Marriage does not mean domestic slavery. To be a good husband you have to be a good man first, and men are not geldings who sit around and only speak when they're spoken to.

Also, it doesn't take much reflection to realize that society would fall apart if most men chose the "wild stallion" option. There would be no families. We'd be murdering each other for access to the best women.

There would be a few really alpha males at the top with most of the women in their harems.

All the collective energy of the male sex drive needs to be focused towards something that maximizes society's resources and builds a prosperous state. In other words, a man's sex drive should push him towards marriage and family, and one very effective way to do that is to have a standard that sex is limited to marriage.

This isn't a matter of prudery, and it doesn't require us to think that sex is bad. Rather, an environment in which men have to get married before they can have sex does all sorts of good for society.

My brother very helpfully defines "culture" as "what a man needs to do to get laid." I think that's a pretty useful way to look at things.

So let's compare what Sherlock Holmes' neighbor had to do to get laid with what a modern resident of Baker Street might have to do.

Sherlock's neighbor had to graduate from school. He had to get a job. He had to "have prospects." He had to win the girl's attention and affection as well as the parents' approval, which probably meant he had to present himself well, have good table manners, speak well, dress well, have a good reputation, and so on. Then he had to go through a sexless courtship and engagement, and once this was all finished he got to marry the girl and have sex on their wedding night.

That sort of a culture keeps young men in check. It provides them with an incentive to make something of themselves.

What does a man have to do today? Hardly anything. No wonder he's content to sit in front of the TV or the Playstation.

The question you should be asking yourself is why a young man should have to do something — anything — before he can get laid. The modern perspective is that it's all about rights and liberties and freedom. People can do whatever they want so long as it doesn't hurt anybody.

That perspective is very naive.

Sex is so available these days because women have lowered their standards. If you haven't seen it yet, go to YouTube and look up "the economics of sex" from the Austin Institute.

When women set the kind of high barrier to sex that I have been recommending — that is, only inside marriage — then it's in all women's best interest to shame the sluts, because when the sluts lower the market value of sex, it hurts every woman and every marriage.

Just because humans have sex in private doesn't mean that sex is entirely a private affair between consenting adults. That is part of the modern delusion. We have sex in private, but the rules governing sex are everybody's business.

The modern approach to sex doesn't build a culture. It doesn't harness the energy of the young man's sex drive to make young men into responsible, useful members of society. It also fails to maximize women's potential as wives and mothers. It is, in short, destroying civilized society.

For the time being our society is living off the borrowed capital of previous generations. A couple more generations of the modern way and we'll be in full-bore idiocracy.

We have this huge reservoir of energy sitting out there. It's called "the male sex drive." And we've wasted it. We haven't used it to create anything, to build our society or to create a positive environment for the next generation. Instead, we glorify rappers who say unspeakable things and act like they belong in prison.

Sex needs to be directed towards something useful, which is marriage and family.

• Birth control changed behavior, but it didn't change human nature

To some people, the idea that sex should be delayed until marriage sounds horribly old-fashioned and completely unnecessary since the invention of birth control. A lot of the "calculus of marriage" I discuss above assumes that sex will result in babies, and with good birth control that isn't always the case. Someone might ask, "Why should we follow rules that were developed in a pre-birth control world?"

I think it's wrong to assume that birth control has changed things that much. The most obvious reason is that human nature didn't suddenly change when they started carrying condoms at CVS. I suppose it's possible that birth control would eventually change human nature, but I think that would take a long time.

Here are some very practical reasons why sex should be delayed until marriage.

1. Birth control isn't perfect. It's far better for a married couple to have an unexpected pregnancy than for two people who hardly know one another.

2. Sometimes women say they're on birth control, get pregnant and use that to hook the man into something he didn't want. Like child support payments.

3. This one is more for the women. If you get naked with some guy, then break up with him, you may find yourself the star on a "revenge porn" site. The larger point (for both sexes) is that physical intimacy needs to come after emotional intimacy and trust. And I don't just mean "do you trust me?" trust. I mean legally enforceable trust.

4. When a man and a woman have sex they experience a series of biochemical reactions that make them feel more lovey dovey. That is, sex causes emotional bonding. Unfortunately, that feeling doesn't tell you if you're a good match or would make a good couple, so if you have any sense you should figure those things out first.

The modern sequence is something like

- attraction
- then sex
- then maybe love
- then maybe marriage.

It's been a disaster, for obvious reasons.

It makes far more sense for the sequence to go

- attraction
- then maybe love
- then maybe marriage
- then sex.

It puts everything on a much firmer foundation. The rule is that marriage is the appropriate context for romantic love. Our culture puts that in reverse — romantic love is the context for marriage. That leads to obvious problems.

• There are good marriages out there

Despite the cultural and legal wasteland that has caused the decline in marriage … despite the raving lunacies of the modern disease … despite a popular culture that takes every opportunity to tear down the foundations of family — there are successful marriages out there, and the people who are in them are extraordinarily happy. I strongly suspect they are much happier than the Men's Rights Advocates or the feminists.

People in good marriages have found something true — that transcends culture and law and the calculus of marriage. They've found what lies at the heart of marriage, which is committed love in the service of something greater.

Earlier I mentioned something called the marriage strike. Some young men have decided that marriage is a raw deal and they have opted out. I don't blame them. Marriage isn't what it used to be. The law and the culture no longer support it, and in many ways they undermine it. But love is still the best thing in life, and committed, life-long love is the best part of love.

I still believe that marriage is a viable option, under carefully controlled circumstances.

If a man is going to marry today, he has to do it the way a man might have bargained in the wild west. He has to be very careful with whom he does business, and he can't count on anybody to come rescue him, or make the deal fair. He has to understand the risks, set the terms of the deal, and go into it eyes wide open.

Conclusion — Why a man should marry

A reasonable case can be made that traditional marriage is an institution that doesn't fit in the modern world. Many of the assumptions that underlie traditional marriage don't seem to apply the same way in this rich, safe world we've created. (I'm speaking to people in the western world. There are still places on the planet where the old rules apply quite well.)

The circumstances of life have changed, but men and women haven't really changed. The same drives and desires that developed over thousands of years still churn and boil in the backs of our minds, subtly influencing our thoughts and actions. Is it possible to fulfill those desires in a sensible way in the modern world — recognizing that men and women are different, but also recognizing that the world is a different place?

I think so, but it's a challenge that has to be faced honestly.

We all need to realize that the law and the culture have changed so much that the average man is incentivized *not to marry* in modern society. There's hardly a reason to take on the yoke. The bargain simply isn't very good any more.

So given all this confusion and trouble, we have to ask what kind of a man should marry, and why? I believe it comes down to a few things. The kind of man who should marry — despite all the obstacles and problems and confusions — is the man who believes these things.

1. Real love involves a life-long commitment.

2. Sex isn't just entertainment.

3. Children should be raised in a positive, healthy environment.

4. Life isn't just about me.

On the first point, why do the women's magazines talk about "getting him to commit?" Because *commitment* is a measure of how serious you are about somebody. Despite all our efforts to pretend that we can dash in and out of relationships, something in the heart still calls out for a commitment to a single person. There is something deep in the heart that says that forever means something more.

Kenny Chesney's own marriage didn't work out very well, but he expressed the longing for commitment in his song: "I wanna know how forever feels."

If you don't feel that way, then marriage is not for you. But if you do, it might be.

On #2, sex isn't like playing tennis, or like watching a good movie. There's a sociological reason for couples who have sex to bond emotionally, and there are biological realities that make it happen. Sex and love are supposed to go together. You can be callous and subdue those feelings if you like, but there are consequences. Your car won't run right on the wrong kind of fuel, and your life won't run right if you try to deny who you are as a person.

If you believe that sex and love belong together in the context of a life-long commitment, then marriage might be for you.

And then there's kids.

Kids are a constant source of worry and frustration. They drain your time and your money. They eat up your food and make a mess of your house.

But you know what? They're worth it. Parents make incredible sacrifices for kids, and they enjoy doing it. If your car is broken, you get another car. If your kid is broken, you move heaven and earth to help him.

You can say this is just a trick. "If parents didn't have this irrational attachment to their young, then the species would not have survived. That feeling you have towards your kids is just your DNA conning you into doing its bidding."

That's right. Everything in life presents the same choice between the chance and the dance. If you want to view your mind as a trick of your biology, go right ahead. But I don't think it will make you happy.

We like to believe that we'll be happy if we look out for ourselves, but it often turns out that we're happier when we look out for others. The self-centered person is often miserable, but sharing your life with others is a proven path to joy.

The man who is fit for marriage is the man who has a vision beyond the statistics, beyond the law, beyond the biology, beyond the just-so stories of the evolutionary psychologists and despite the crazy views that are popular in our culture. He's the man who believes in love, in virtue, and in family. He is counter-cultural in a way the hippies couldn't have imagined.

Because of that he has to be *very careful* in choosing a mate. He needs to find a woman who hasn't been soaked in the cultural cocktail of equalitarianism and related foolishness. He has to plan to live his life by a different set of values, and in a subculture that supports them. The broader culture will not. It will be his enemy.

The marrying man also realizes the difference between love and infatuation. "Falling in love" is fun and exciting, but that's not what long-term love is about. Long-term love is a commitment, and it takes effort to make it work.

If that's you, then bless you, and good luck.

END

Resources

If you want to explore this topic a little further, try some of these resources. I don't completely agree with any of them, but they are helpful.

The Art of Manliness blog.

The Dalrock blog, and the blogs he links to in the right column.

Watch the "Girlwriteswhat" videos on Youtube. You might start with "What, me a feminist?"

The War on Men by Suzanne Venker

The Myth of Male Power by Warren Farrell.

Married Man Sex Life by Athol Kay.

If you enjoyed this book .... Independent authors rely on our readers to spread the word about our books, so if you enjoyed this work *please* give it a positive review on Amazon.com, tell your Facebook friends and otherwise spread the word.

About the Author

Greg Krehbiel is a happily married father of five wonderful children. He's had a distinguished career in professional publishing, including lengthy gigs in editorial, product development, IT and tech development, marketing, and audio and web conferencing. He has a degree in Geology and studied theology as preparation for ministry — then thought better of it. He's a home brewer (beer, wine and mead), an occasional jogger, a swing dancer, an avid writer, and enjoys camping and fishing. You can contact Greg directly at gkrehbiel@gmail.com.

Other Books by Greg Krehbiel

The Hidden Village - This exciting urban fantasy is set in and around Washington, D.C. Geof Franklin gets the late-night call every parent fears. His son's car has been involved in a serious accident and Alek has gone missing. As Geof looks for clues to his son's whereabouts, he uncovers two mysterious "worlds within worlds" right in the middle of the city. Hidden Village, a fun and engaging computer game, turns out to be the doorway to a system of dangerous clans. The clansmen are people with very rare abilities and personal characteristics who live their own secretive lives, by their own rules, and think nothing of breaking the law or the people who get in their way.

The Five Lives of John and Jillian - Cross *The Time Traveler's Wife* with a classic Alfred Hitchcock movie, add the concept of a multiverse and you have an idea what to expect in *The Five Lives of John and Jillian.* What would happen to star-crossed lovers in an alternate universe? John and Jillian seem destined to cross paths and fall in love, but every time they meet the story is different, and malevolent forces intervene to keep them apart.

In *The Witch's Promise,* cynical John meets and falls in love with a beautiful Wiccan. His orderly, rational world comes apart as he's confronted with a world of tarot card readings, pagan revelries, waking dreams and visions. In *The Witch's Bastard* their relationship takes a turn for the worst and John struggles to keep his distance and his sanity. *What God Has Bent* takes us to happier times in the lives of the young lovers, but a dangerous secret from Jillian's past threatens to derail their future together. In *Pipe Dreams,* John is sliding into depression and alcoholism from his grief over the death of his love. Now the mysterious discovery of his grandfather's pipe has awakened something in his mind and he's begun to have lucid dreams, which have progressed to daytime visions that threaten to drive him mad. Can he find the secret of the pipe and reunite with Jillian? *A Collision of Worlds* wraps up the stories with John and Jillian seemingly enjoying a happy marriage, but a secret force conspires to drive them apart. And Jillian's life is on the line.

The Intruder - Jeremy Mitchell is a refugee from a separatist, anti-technology community who is a fish out of water in the high-tech society of the 21st century. He recklessly plunges himself into his new environment and finds himself caught in a confusing web of technology and intrigue. Powerful forces try to make him a pawn in a contest between rival intelligence organizations, but he doesn't play along with their game and makes his own rules. His loyalties are tested by a budding love affair with a young college student, who, along with her computer geek girlfriend, are unintentionally pulled into the conflict.

Merlin's Last Days - Born of a mysterious and powerful woman from an ancient line of pagan rulers, Merrell Anthony believes that it's his destiny to put Arthur Pendragon on the emperor's throne in Rome and set the world on a more secure path. Being born in 1965 must not get in his way. When Marianne Gallagher storms into Merrell's life at a small college town in Pennsylvania, she exhibits hints of the same gift that allows Merrell to project his mind into the body of a 6th century druid as Merlin the Mage. As Merrill and Marianne carry on an illicit love affair, tensions grow from their contradictory views on the future of the Pendragon — and the proper path for all humanity. (Note: this book is *not* suitable for children.)

About Crowhill Publishing

"Krehbiel" is a German name that roughly translates to English as "Crow Hill." Or so I'm told. Crowhill Publishing is the imprint for all of Greg Krehbiel's books. Find out more at http://crowhill-publishing.com.

Printed in Great Britain
by Amazon